11/19/16

MW00437468

Never Left the Battlefields

Birney T. "Chick" Havey

Clovercroft Publishing

Never Left the Battlefields

© 2015 by Birney T. Havey

Published by Clovercroft Publishing, Franklin, Tennessee

Cover and Interior Design by Suzanne Lawing

Edited by Bob Irvin

Background photo by Filip Ghinea - Photography Chronicles

Printed in the United States of America

978-1-940262-87-1

Contents

ACKNOWLEDGMENTS

My sincerest gratitude goes to longtime friend Joe Machol, who, as I wrote in this book, has caught "the bug" of honoring war service, and possesses a passionate desire to help chronicle the actions of those who served in World War II. Joe has served me in so many ways, including twice traveling to Europe with me. I owe a great deal of gratitude to Joe.

To publisher Larry Carpenter of Christian Book Services. Larry is an incredibly skilled publisher and visionary. Many thanks to Larry for believing in this project.

And to editor Bob Irvin, who skillfully wove the many pieces together. Bob helped write at times, followed the book map I gave him to a T, and yet added great creativity and his own passion for this project. My deepest thanks to Bob as well.

WHY I WROTE THIS BOOK

After viewing and reading so many war stories, with most having many inaccuracies, and with the urging of my friends and relatives, I finally decided to write this book. My hope is that it will bring forth a more factual story of the events and history of the end of World War II, from my perspective, a private soldier on the ground with all of the misery and witness of combat and war.

The Winter of 1944-1945 in Europe caused the suffering of thousands of our troops and the local civilians, along with the privation, suffering, and death caused by Hitler's armies. The force of the German assault could have brought them world domination, and with the Japanese assault on our west coast, we might well have lost our country as we know it. Surely our president, Franklin Roosevelt, with his foresight, must be given credit for saving not only our United States but also most of the free world. He did so, of course, alongside England's Winston Churchill.

Therefore, I was compelled to tell my story, and I offer it to you here.

Birney T. "Chick" Havey
Seabrook, Texas
February 2015

CAMP CARSON;
FORT BENNING

Camp Carson was where I trained for war.

Carson was located just west and a bit south of Colorado Springs, on the slope of Cheyenne Mountain, in sight of the famous Pikes Peak, a 14,100-foot high mountain. This was a summer resort area built in the 1930s, a wasteland area of about 50 square miles later selected for Carson.

The gigantic resources of the U.S. Government were thrown into building this city for about 100,000 men and various services supporting their training. All around it, there are high valleys and draws leading up to the much higher Pikes Peak. In fact, the Cheyenne Mountain Air Force Station is located there now, near a North American Aerospace Defense Command (NORAD) installation.

The big defense contractors were still building quarters for troops when I arrived, a recruit of about 19 or 20 (I'm not sure which), a young man shaving once a month whether I needed it or not! (I took a lot of kidding about that.) I was assigned to the 69th Division Headquarters; this was because I had an above-average IQ test result. My mechanical test result was super; in fact, the guy behind me copied my mechanical test paper. When I saw him some weeks later he was assigned to the division headquarters motor pool and was even in line to head up that motor pool. Me? I was assigned to the division as a statistician, calling for a warrant officer's grade.

The division was being formed during the spring and summer of 1942. In short, this was an amazing enterprise that could be produced by the might of the United States—to build infantry quarters for a division of some 25,000 men is beyond understanding. It was astounding: within a year, hundreds of large, two-story barracks, a water system, sewers, drains, stores, PXs (post exchanges), theaters, rifle ranges, parade grounds—all covering miles and miles of roads and fencing. And Carson was only one of some twenty such installations! I ask you, what other country in the world had the skill and might to do such a thing?

Now, when I say the camp is located in a wasteland . . . well, rumors have it that the early Indians would not go there because of the Rocky Mountain Spotted Fever ticks and the deadly fever caused by a tick bite.

With rattlesnakes and other difficulties, the deep-cut arroyos were not too good for grazing cattle or sheep. It was a dry, prairie dog strip of land. The arroyos were some 12 to 20 feet across and 10 to 30 feet deep; they were, in fact, big natural drainage ditches, miles long, causing the troops long detours around them.

Some of the guys, though, would take a dare to jump across those deep ditches, thus saving miles of marching. And if you successfully jumped across, you could get in a nap of an hour or so, or at least a break. But those gulley sidewalls were too steep to climb up or down and were made of rocky gray clay worn by years of flash flood water cascading down from rainstorms. In jumping, we had to carry our equipment, boots, cartridge belt, rifle, and more, and sometimes a raincoat—and it took a good approach run. I could jump across about 12 feet.

TRAINING HIKES

Our training detail included conditioning and company training. We would hike out about 10 to 12 miles and then eat lunch sandwiches with some water from our canteens, which held about a pint. Keep in mind, it is July and August. It was quite hot and dry on that plain, but you would hardly sweat due to the dry mountain air. There were no trees, just cactuses and weeds with prairie dog holes and big rocks.

We were told in our infantry training that if you walk at 120 steps per minute with a ten-minute rest, you can cover about two and a half miles an hour; if it was rough terrain, about two miles an hour. This is not necessarily fast, but just a good pace of walking. So heading out at 7 AM, four hours would get you about nine miles out from your starting point. We would then spend one-half hour for lunch and rest, and then hike back.

Each trip required different equipment loads. I recall one particular day out on the plain when we had just finished lunch. A big, black thunderstorm blew over us from the mountains, just a few miles to our west. It soon rained so hard we were ankle-deep in water. And then it began to hail: at first, small pellets, then growing larger and larger, to golf ball-size and larger. Dangerous hail.

We had no cover, so we had to lay down in the mud and water and try to cover our heads with our rifle stocks; we wore only fatigue soft hats, fatigue suits, cartridge belts, and leggings and boots. The large hailstones beat the hell out of us, and after a good pasting the hail continued, but then became pea size, covering the ground all around us six inches deep in hail. Some in our detail were badly injured, and ambulances were hauling them out. We all were badly bruised, knots all over our heads, and after we got back to our barracks, military doctors examined us. They applied alcohol to our bruises, and we received two days off to recover. Everyone looked black and blue for days.

But that was just a part of our training. The war was going on, and we were trying to get ready for it. All in all, the weather was really not too bad; winters could be cold, but it also could warm up to 60 degrees on some days.

> THE LARGE HAILSTONES BEAT THE HELL OUT OF US, AND AFTER A GOOD PASTING THE HAIL CONTINUED, BUT THEN BECAME PEA SIZE, COVERING THE GROUND ALL AROUND US SIX INCHES DEEP IN HAIL. SOME IN OUR DETAIL WERE BADLY INJURED, AND AMBULANCES WERE HAULING THEM OUT.

* * * * *

One of my first jobs while troops were arriving was being in charge of a detail of men; our job was to line the deep ditches with rock and plants and trees. I had two two-and-a-half-ton trucks, with six men to a truck. Our job was to go up into the hills, load up stones, haul them down, and then line the ditches in about a ten-square-blocks area. The job turned out pretty good. It looked military, and the commanding general was pleased.

Next, I was then sent back to headquarters with my statistician job; my work was to begin sorting out men in different categories. I had this simple thought: *This is not how I want to fight a war.* So I was looking for a way to get busy.

I asked for and received a transfer to one of the three infantry regiments of the 69th Division, and there I began training with the company, doing all the basic requirements: rifle shooing, pistol firing, hand grenade throwing, bayonet fighting, hand-to-hand combat, carbine firing, first aid, knife combat. For all of these, I received high grades. So they made me a corporal and gave me a squad of twelve men in a platoon.

My company commander called me into his office and told me they were looking for officer candidates; the school was at Fort Benning, Georgia. I applied and was accepted.

I'll never forget leaving Camp Carson in the back of an Army two-and-a-half-ton truck. The sunset over the mountains was striking as we pulled away; I was alone in the back of the truck. Birney Havey was off to a new adventure.

FORT BENNING: OFFICER CADET SCHOOL

The officer training, called OCS (Officer Cadet School), was for ninety days. It was very hard work and very disciplined; everything had to be perfect. Your bunk, your dress, everything.

THEY WERE TRAINING US TO KILL THE ENEMY—BUT TO BE GENTLEMEN ABOUT IT.

We were only allowed passes to town twice. They had a demerit system similar to West Point, including an honor system with rigid rules.

They were training us to kill the enemy—but to be gentlemen about it.

Even the eating and mess rules were strict. There were rules on the proper handling of food—you could not dip into food when passing across the table to another—sitting up straight, using your napkin, and more. The field training was excellent; we had artillery and mortar training. We were trained and tested and retested. I was greatly impressed.

At one class we all sat in an outdoor grandstand. The instructors had parked directly in front of us a big 155-mm artillery gun. Being infantrymen, it was good training to know all about our support weapons, their routine and firing procedures, the aiming and calculating, and so forth. The 155-mm cannon would fire out for a distance of 15 miles, usually just over our heads, hitting the enemy out in front of us while advancing. The artillery instructor had us stand directly behind the big cannon, from which they fired off a big shell. It was hard to believe you could actually see that big projectile fly out a big, round black spot in the air. As it flies forward and out it becomes a smaller spot and then disappears on its way forward. We now have jet fighter planes that move at the same speed, or faster.

This Army method of teaching in OCS was unique; their methods of teaching theory, visual, and hands-on application was phenomenal, a way to teach whole groups, in a limited time, to expand and develop one army—this could only happen in the USA.

Moving toward the last two weeks, they sprang an Army test on us—even after we had been measured and had picked out our new, fine-tailored officer uniforms. The surprise test did not concern our activity in the infantry school, but were all about extracurricular subjects. I did not score well, and flunked.

A review board sent me back to my original post at Camp Carson, Colorado. I could have started out with a new class, but I chose not to do that.

Back in Colorado, I chose to go to the Parachute School, so back off to Fort Benning I went! There, I went through "jump school," a six-week, physically intense course with multiple stages. It culminated with the "D" stage, which marked your fifth jump at night. We received fifty bucks per month extra as long as we qualified on jump status (this was one jump every three months).

I was chosen to remain at the school as an assistant jump instructor; this was during the era where the 101st Division was but a regiment and not yet expanded to a division.

SUMMER 1944

It was now the summer of 1944. The North Africa invasion had occurred, the invasion of Europe was forthcoming, and I was missing the war.

I was told by my superiors that I could go to the pool as a replacement, where I would go to the next division shipping out overseas.

That is how I went directly to the 42nd "Rainbow" Division at Camp Gruber, Oklahoma. I was on my way to war. Little did I know what lay ahead. I had miles to go, but I was also well trained in the art of war.

THE STORY OF
THE RAINBOW

It's important to know a portion of the background of the unit that I followed into war. This is part of the story of its second birth—its rebirth, if you will. This is excerpted from an official Army publication, *42nd Rainbow Infantry Division: World War II History*.[1]

It was a hot, bright July day when the Rainbow Division, the most famous fighting organization of World War II, was reactivated at Camp Gruber, Oklahoma. The date was July 14, 1943. This was the 26th anniversary of the Battle of Champagne and veterans of the Rainbow who had stopped the last great offensive of the Kaiser's army in that battle were on hand to see their unit reborn.

Here was history repeating itself. Once again there was a Rainbow Division in the U.S. Army, and this time, even more than before, it was a division that would represent all of America, one made up of men selected from each state of the Union in proportion to its population.

The first Rainbow Division was composed of National Guard units from 27 states and it was this collection of men that inspired General Douglas MacArthur, its most famous member, to declare: "The 42nd Infantry Division stretches like a Rainbow from one end of America to the other."

Major General Harry J. Collins, then Brigadier General, recalled the words of General MacArthur on that activation day when he told the veterans of the old Rainbow and the cadremen of the new:

The Rainbow stretches across the land and represents the people of our country. This Division cannot fail because America cannot fail.

The cadremen for the new Rainbow were for the most part regular army men who had been stationed in Hawaii and Newfoundland. They had spent a short time with the 102nd Infantry Division and had been augmented by some officers and men from that unit. They knew their business, but to brush up on fundamentals and teaching methods they attended schools until the first of the fillers began arriving in mid-August, and then everyone went to work to build a 15,000-man fighting team.

TRAINING, TRANSFERS, AND REPLACEMENTS

Basic training began, officially, on October 4, 1943, and the Division received an overall rating of "very satisfactory" in the individual training tests that were conducted during the first week of January. The unit training period was begun on January 9, but shortly thereafter the entire Division training program was disrupted by repeated instructions that men who qualified for overseas shipment be transferred to other units.

Most seriously affected by these transfers from the Division were the three infantry regiments, which shipped out more than 5,000 men in the period from the beginning of the unit training program until the first week of April 1944. During the months that followed more and more men were transferred from the Rainbow and they were replaced with men from army specialist training schools, from the air forces, and from branches of the service other than the infantry. Some of these replacements had no sooner been given short refresher courses in basic training than they too were transferred.

Although the infantry suffered the majority of the transfers, all units were affected, and it was not until late in July that the Division was again able to begin an uninterrupted training program. During the period from early January to the first of September, the Rainbow transferred out and received as replacements more than 15,000 men, a number equal to the strength of the Division.

In July, the Division received assurances that it would not be called upon for more replacements. Instead, it was informed, it must begin an intensive training program that would prepare it for shipment overseas in 26 weeks. Everything must be completed in that time: basic training, unit and combat training, maneuvers, post-maneuver training, and even packing and crating.

This meant that what was normally a year to a year and a half's work must be done in six months.

> EVERYTHING MUST BE COMPLETED IN THAT TIME: BASIC TRAINING, UNIT AND COMBAT TRAINING, MANEUVERS, POST-MANEUVER TRAINING, AND EVEN PACKING AND CRATING. THIS MEANT THAT WHAT WAS NORMALLY A YEAR TO A YEAR AND A HALF'S WORK MUST BE DONE IN SIX MONTHS.

The job was tremendous. Everything had to be shortened, condensed, speeded up. Individual training for the latest group of replacements was cut to six weeks. Unit training was reduced to the same period of time. All tests had to be taken and all POM requirements completed. The Division was working night and day on a seven-day week.

Then came a further change. Infantrymen were needed in Europe immediately. Twenty-six weeks was now too long. . . . Things became even more intense as training was escalated even further.

Birney T. Havey: Official Bio

And now something about myself, and some of the influences on my life, before going off to war.

I was born December 13, 1921, 93 years ago. Being born so late in the year often fools you into thinking you are a year younger than you are.

I was born in St. Louis, Missouri, on Paris Avenue. This was actually North St. Louis and was, ironically, a sort of German settlement, with the Italian section in South St. Louis on Dago Hill. Yogi Berra and Joe Garagiola, of baseball fame (catchers both), came from "the Hill."

I was the only boy, with three sisters, Jane, Violet, and Betty. My grade schools were Ashland and Benton and my high schools Beaumont and Hadley. I started the study of business administration at Washington University, but this was interrupted by World War II.

I joined the U.S. Air Corps, in reserve, in spring 1942, and then volunteered to join the Army, unassigned. I received serial number 17075652 and waited for flying school. But the army had other plans and switched me to the 69th Division, Camp Carson, near Colorado Springs.

My military training was as follows: I had basic training with the 69th Division at Carson, and Officers Training at Fort Benning, Georgia. I then returned to the 69th Division at Carson, but then volunteered to go to Parachute School, which sent me back at Benning.

I became a training instructor (corporal) and requested a transfer to an overseas assigned division.

I joined the 42nd Division, 222nd Infantry, in October 1944.

I completed basic and final training again, and then shipped into the European Theater of Operations (ETO) in November 1944.

We landed in the south of France in November 1944, and this is where war started for Birney Havey.

This book tells of what I experienced during the war.

What became of my life after the war? After the war and my arrival back home in St. Louis, I continued retailing school through a program with Washington University and the May Company. I was received on-the-job training with pay while still seeking my business admin B.A.

I went on to work for my sister, Jane Havey; she owned a real estate business. I became interested in restaurant and bar equipment, along with design; this was the late 1940s.

MID-LIFE AND INTO LATER YEARS

The 1950s and '60s were a loss as I was suffering from combat stress. It was like nothing mattered; this was later diagnosed by the Vets hospital, but not as post-traumatic stress disorder, as people know it today. They had not come up with that description at that time. I think that, in truth, time somewhat mitigated that disorder in my life.

I rode a tidal wave of success in designing and installing bakeries, delis, and restaurants in supermarkets. I built my own warehouse in Topeka, Kansas, and married a young nurse.

I later retired and built a home in Galveston, Texas. Married again in 1978, I fathered two girls, raised them while un-retiring, and opened a restaurant, Texas Shrimp House. I also have worked in these arenas: sales and engineering consulting, help designing Astro Hall (where large rodeos are held), and I worked in kitchen and dining facilities. I later would retire again.

As for my two sweet girls, Crista Havey Grimwood was my oldest. She has two Masters degrees and teaches in Kansas; she also has a yogurt shop. She has two grandkids of mine: Avery and Adin. Jamie Havey Ford, my youngest daughter, has recently been certified as a paramedic and is a nurse at the Bay Area Regional Hospital in Houston. Her husband is a deputy constable, Mike Ford.

Today I live in Seabrook, Texas, where I am still in the restaurant business. I love to quail hunt and fish. And I am writing my book in 2014—I guess it's never too late—70 years after I entered the war, 69 years after the war ended in Europe. Time passes very fast.

OFFICIAL WAR HISTORY

I was in the Battle of the Bulge and the invasion of Germany.

I received a Silver Star, three Bronze Stars, a Purple Heart, three Battle Stars (13 Decorations), Combat Infantry Badge, and Presidential Unit Citation.

I was discharged in January 1946.

Basic Training: 1942, Camp Carson, Colorado
Officers School: 1943, Fort Benning, Georgia
Parachute School: 1943, Fort Benning, Georgia
42nd Division: 1944, Camp Gruber, Muskogee, Oklahoma

St. Louis

Now allow me to go into a little more detail on those early years.

I was born on that December 1921 day at home on Paris Avenue, in the north part of St. Louis. My mother was Anna Rhinehimmer Havey, and my father was Birney Havey Sr., a salesman for Rice Stix Merchandise Company on Washington Avenue in St. Louis. He sold men's and women's ready-to-wear items to retail stores in and around St. Louis.

I was the second child of four, with three sisters. During my childhood in the 1920s, which was before radio and today's automobile, I remember my dad bringing home a borrowed crystal radio (a simple radio in the 1920s, and a rarity) with a single earphone. We were able to listen to the Jack Dempsey-Gene Tunney heavyweight championship prizefight from New York

City. My dad even let me have that single earphone to hear a few words describing the fight. Wow!

I still remember that simple radio device, built on a wood base, 6 inches by 12 inches and one-half-inch thick. The rock crystal was a bright stone, round and wedge-shaped, with a bright sparkling top face, held in a copper stand upright. The other part was set up next to the crystal, kind of a feeler with a spiraled wire end and a music type of stinger; this was called a cat's whisker. It had an up-and-down swivel-action device with a single nonpowered earphone, and it didn't require any type of electricity. Using the cat's whisker, we could lightly dig around on the face of the upright crystal until we found music or a station. Later, kits were sold to make up your own set, even after the invention of the radio tube. What memories!

In 1928, my dad took me out to Lambert's Field Airport to see Charles Lindbergh's airplane right before he flew across the Atlantic Ocean. I was six years old. We drove out the Natural Bridge Road to the airfield where Lindbergh's plane was parked by a brown brick building. We didn't have airlines back then, so there was no ticket office; there were no stands. We went out to a large concrete slab area called the tarmac, where Lindbergh had his plane tied down. It was out in the open, with no guards, fencing, or any type of security. How times have changed!

A few people were walking around and looking the plane over. A few days later, Lindbergh flew to New York and then on to France . . . and right on into fame! Years later, our 42nd Division held its reunion at the Marriott, which was right next to the street where Lindbergh parked his plane. I told the antitank boys and my service mates my story about Lindbergh's plane, and they were in awe. (The 42nd Division later held their annual reunion in St. Louis.)

42ND REUNION, ST. LOUIS—MORE THAN FORTY YEARS LATER

About the same time as this reunion, my wife, Kim, and I had just built a new home in Galveston, Texas, right on the bay. Our two children, Crista and Jamie, were at a summer camp in North Texas. I received news of the 42nd Division reunion being held in my old hometown of St. Louis. I told Kim that we should head up for it. I knew a lot of the good food places like Schnedhorst in Clayton and a place called Ragazzis, out on the hill, to name a few. The next day, we took off for that Marriott. We signed in at the reunion and started looking out for my old company members.

The first one I ran into was Jack Westbrook and his wife. The last time I saw Jack was during an attack in the Vosges Mountains below Strasbourg in February 1945. Jack had just been wounded by shrapnel in the back. He was bleeding through his stretcher canvas, blood oozing onto the ground. My squad and I were passing through his platoon on the way up to a firefight. I remember that I asked him if I could do anything for him, as he was all alone, just waiting to be carried out. Lying there, he said, "No thanks." And that was the last time I saw or even heard about him—until now, all these years later in St. Louis.

Everyone enjoyed my young wife, Kim. She was very attractive with a great personality. One of the strange things about the event was two out of every three guys there had never attended a 42nd Division reunion before. St. Louis was a central location for a regional meeting, however, allowing more folks to come. Captain George Waters and his wife, Shirley, came all the way from Rome, New York. They had become publishers of the Rome newspaper.

McEndorfer (he was called Mac, of course) was a lieutenant and platoon leader before he was wounded. He established a home with his wife in El Paso, Texas. What a privilege to see him. Apparently, his dad left him a large pecan grove in El Paso. He did quite well for himself, selling off a large parcel for a housing development. Later, I flew the entire family out for a vacation, and Mac visited us; we would enjoy excellent seafood and he enjoyed a break from all the dust.

> CALL IT WHATEVER YOU WANT, BUT MOST SOLDIERS CARRIED AROUND A HEAVY BURDEN OF GUILT. THE KICKER WAS WE REALLY DIDN'T REALIZE IT—NOT UNTIL THAT DAY WHEN WE OPENLY TALKED ABOUT THE WAR.

Lieutenant Russ Fielding, who also lived in Rome, New York, worked for George Waters at the *Rome Sentinel*. Fielding too had been wounded in action. He was at the 42nd Division reunion as well, and the atmosphere at this gathering was quite euphoric! But we also had to deal with some things. All the guys held a private meeting in one of our hotel rooms and got things off our chests. We spoke about our adventures and the killings on both sides—things some of us hadn't spoken of in more than forty years. Surprisingly, sharing with one another alleviated the remnants of post-traumatic stress disorder (PTSD) that some of us no doubt still carried with us. Back in our day, we didn't have such a term. Call it whatever you want, but most soldiers carried around a heavy burden of guilt. The kicker was we really didn't realize it—not until that day when we openly talked about the war.

Our conversation and time together seemed to open us up, and we could freely talk about our deeds of war, knowing no man would be judged. Most people have never lived through such a sustained and lengthy combat situation, with their lives on the line, daily, like the men from WWII. That we could each move past all that death and go on to live our lives is pretty astounding.

Between dead comrades, killed enemy, and prison death camps, I saw more dead, starved, mangled, and mutilated bodies than lived in my entire hometown!

What follows are many of those stories.

A century later, WWI's impact reverberates around globe

Great War shifted power, reshaped map, destroyed empires

ZONNEBEKE, Belgium — To walk the orderly rows of headstones in the elegant graveyards that hold the dead of World War I is to feel both awe and distance. With the death of the last veterans, World War I, which began 100 years ago, has moved from memory to history. But its resonance has not faded — on land and geography, people and nations, and on the causes and consequences of modern war.

The memorial here at Tyne Cot, near Ypres and the muddy killing ground of Passchendaele, is the largest British Commonwealth cemetery in the world. Nearly 12,000 soldiers are buried here — some 8,400 of them identified only as "A Soldier of the Great War, Known Unto God." Despite the immensity of this space, the soldiers represent only a tiny portion of the 8.5 million or more from both sides who died.

In Europe's first total war, called the Great War until the second one came along, 7 million civilians also died.

World War I could be said to have begun in Sarajevo on June 28, 1914, with the assassination of Archduke Franz Ferdinand and his wife, Sophie, by a young nationalist seeking a greater Serbia. The 4½ years that followed, as the war spread throughout Europe, the Middle East and Asia, reshaped the modern world in fundamental ways.

The war destroyed kings and czars, it demolished empires, it introduced chemical weapons, tanks and airborne bombing. It brought millions of women into the workforce, hastening their legal right to vote. It gave independence to

Tomas Munita /The New York Times
The U.S. 42nd Division memorial is at the site of the 1918 Battle of Croix Rouge Farm in France. The assassination that triggered World War I happened 100 years ago today.

nations like Ukraine, Poland and the Baltic countries and created new nations in the Middle East with often arbitrary borders. It brought about major cultural changes, including a new understanding of what was then called "shell shock."

It also featured the initial step of the U.S. as a global power. And the rapid retreat of the U.S. from Europe helped sow the ground for World War II.

Historians still squabble over responsibility for the war. Some continue to blame Germany, and others depict a system of rivalries, alliances and anxieties, driven by concerns about the growing weakness of the Austro-Hungarian and Ottoman empires and the growing strength of Germany and Russia that was likely to produce a war in any case, even if there was some other immediate cause.

But the emotional legacies are different for different countries. For France the war, however bloody, was a necessary response to invasion. Preventing the German army from reaching Paris in the first battle of the Marne spelled the difference between freedom and slavery. The second battle of the Marne, with the help at last of U.S. soldiers, was the beginning of the end for the Germans. This was France's "good war," while World War II was an embarrassing collapse, with significant collaboration.

For Germany, which had invested heavily in the machinery of war, it was an almost incomprehensible defeat, laying the groundwork for revolution, fascism and genocide. Oddly enough, says Max Hastings, a war historian, Germany could have dominated Europe in 20 years economically if only it had not gone to war.

For Britain, there remains a debate about whether the British even had to fight. But fight they did, with millions of volunteers until the dead were mounded so high that conscription was finally imposed in 1916. The memory of July 1,

1916, the first day of the Battle of the Somme — when 20,000 British soldiers died, 40,000 were wounded and 60 percent of officers were killed — has marked British consciousness and become a byword for mindless slaughter.

"The sense that the war was futile and unnecessary still hangs over a lot of the discussion in Britain," said Lawrence Freedman, professor of war studies at King's College, London.

The poppy is one of the most obvious inheritances of the Great War — made famous in the 1915 poem by a Canadian military doctor, Lt. Col. John McCrae: "In Flanders fields, the poppies blow, between the crosses row on row, that mark our place." The short poem was written as a eulogy and a call to solidarity from the dead to the living, that they not "break faith with us who die."

Not far away is the tiny Flanders Field American Cemetery and Memorial, an exquisitely kept six acres containing only 368 graves, including 21 unknown, while the names of 43 more, missing in action, are carved on the walls of a small chapel.

Steven Erlanger,
The New York Times

I was moved by this Dallas Morning News *article on the carnage of World War I—and the 100th anniversary of what began the two great wars in Europe. This was published June 28, 2014.*

MISSOURI RECRUITING DISTRICT
UNITED STATES ARMY RECRUITING SERVICE
624 New Federal Building
St. Louis, Missouri

13 June, 1942

Dear Sir:

Under a recent ruling of the War Department, on the basis of the grade which you made on the Aviation Cadet Mental Screening test, you are eligible to apply for enlistment in the Army of the United States for Glider Pilot training.

This is a two months course, the successful completion of which will bring a rating of Staff-Sergeant. Selected graduates of the Army Air Forces Glider Schools will be appointed Officers in the Army of the United States. Demonstration of soldierly qualities of leadership, judgement, force and discipline will be the criteria upon which such appointments are based.

For further information and details, it is suggested that you contact this office in the very near future.

Trusting we will have the pleasure of seeing you in the near future, let's

KEEP 'EM FLYING

W. S. Mitchell, Jr.

W. S. MITCHELL, JR.,
1st Lieut., F.A.
Asst. Rctg. Officer.

The Missouri Recruiting District wrote to me in June 1942. I was eligible for enlistment in the Army (glider pilot training)! They often ended these letters with the familiar tagline: "Keep 'Em Flying.

AVIATION CADET EXAMINING BOARD
624 New Federal Building
Saint Louis, Missouri

July 30, 1942

Birney T. Havey, Jr.
4629 Margaretta
St. Louis, Missouri
Dear Sir:

Our records indicate that you left your name as a prospective Glider Pilot. Recent instructions are to the effect that men without flying experience sufficient to qualify them as Class A Glider Pilots will receive their training under the Civilian Pilot Training program and that no additional quotas will be assigned this office for enlistment of Class B Glider Pilots.

The Army may resume the direct training of Class B Glider Pilots in the future but it is suggested that you write for information to one of the following addresses:

Civilian Pilot Training
Box 68 Lambert Field Branch
St. Louis, Missouri

or

Civil Aeronautics Administration
9th Floor City Hall
Kansas City, Missouri

Let's "KEEP 'EM FLYING."

W. S. Mitchell Jr.
W. S. MITCHELL, JR.
1st Lt., FA
Asst. Recruiting Officer.

The Aviation Cadet Examining Board wrote to me in July of 1942. I was told I would need to go through civilian pilot training to get my necessary certification.

WORLD WAR II
BIRNEY HAVEY
42ND DIVISION
222ND INFANTRY
AT. COMPANY
SILVER STAR
BRONZE STAR (2)
PURPLE HEART
3 BATTLE STARS
BATTLE OF NORTH FRANCE
BATTLE OF THE BULGE
INVASION OF GERMANY

COMBAT INFANTRY BADGE

BIRNEY HAVEY

BATTLE OF THE BULGE AND TASK FORCE LINDEN

We were off to war. After arriving in Marseilles, France in the last part of November, we, the 222nd Infantry Regiment, were assembled just north of Marseilles in a camp called CP2 (for Command Post 2).

We all put up our pup tents and dug in; there were air raids each night, just around midnight. As you might imagine, both days and nights were turning colder. This was the prelude to a brutal winter, so it was getting cold quick. We just didn't know the deprivations and cold we were yet to face.

Then came the German attack in Belgium famously known as the Battle of the Bulge. It began on the 16th of December, 1944.

Our 222nd was moved into action two days later. We were assigned to Patton's Third Army, and we moved out via two-and-a-half-ton trucks for Belgium and Luxembourg. As we headed out, we could feel it becoming colder, first with rain and then rain changing to snow. We suffered greatly during the two days en route as the temps dropped below the teens. We were leaving Nancy, France, and there was mud everywhere.

I will never forget the 19th and 20th of December. We stopped for what was termed piss call, right in a small village. Some folks came out of the village shops with pitchers of red-hot chicken bouillon, and we each got nearly a half-canteen of that hot soup. Heavenly, it was so good. We asked where we were, and we were told we were in the town of Esch Sur in Luxembourg.

> SOME FOLKS CAME OUT OF THE VILLAGE SHOPS WITH PITCHERS OF RED-HOT CHICKEN BOUILLON, AND WE EACH GOT NEARLY A HALF-CANTEEN OF THAT HOT SOUP.

I was amazed that we had passed out of France. We could then start to hear the sounds of artillery as we passed into Belgium the morning of the 21st. We unloaded out into the snow and fog onto a road covered with troops; now the big shells were getting closer—both theirs and ours. The tanks were starting and stopping, but we marched forward, passing them in columns of twos, always moving toward the gunfire.

We were becoming worn down, as we had had no decent sleep for five days other than in the trucks, sitting up. If we only knew how much fatigue was coming, but we didn't know it then. At dark we spread out, set up our defense, dug in, and got some rest—four hours on duty and then four hours off to rest, with K rations and water. There were no fires; the fog had set in and it was still snowing.

The next morning we hit the road at dawn, where we hit the left flank of von Rundstedt's German attacking army's patrols. We formed skirmish lines and went into our very first firefight of the war. No one in my outfit expressed any fear. We had some targets, along a hedge line, of white, camouflaged German infantry. We poured rifle and machine gun fire on them and that was it; we killed four and wounded six in that first skirmish battle, as I recall. I remember looking over the bodies, and we continued on our advance for the rest of that day.

That evening, we were ordered relieved and marched back over that same route. We met up with trucks and headed for Strasbourg, the capital of Alsace-Lorraine, back in France. We ended that day in the town of St. Hubert, Belgium. We did not know what day it was, but we knew it was close to Christmas, like two days before.

This was our initial push, and this was among the efforts needed to stop the German attack, known as Nordwind, or the Battle of the Bitche Bulge. (Bitche was a nearby city.) And that was the last of the well-known Task Force Linden, which had done its job.

An interesting postscript: As we joined up with our 42nd Division Seventh Army, we removed the Third Army uniform patches that had been sewn on. We sewed back on our 42nd Division Rainbow patches . . . and we did so in the cold, with thread and needle and our bare hands! We had to be masters of sewing, too. Can you even imagine that?

A soldier drew this profile of me in 1945.

It was called Invasion Money. This is five francs.
I still have the original 5-franc bill.

WINTER
1944/1945

NORTH FRANCE, BELGIUM

The winter of 1944-1945 in Northern France and Belgium was one of the coldest, with a fury of fog and snowfall. They said this winter broke records. Before talking about specific battles and actions, it's helpful to understand just how bitter that winter was.

Being from the Midwest, I had experienced bitter cold winter weather before. I had seen plenty of cold fronts move in, bringing the temperature down to twenty below zero (Fahrenheit) for a couple of days, then bouncing back up to normal winter temps (around 32 degrees). Snow that fell overnight melting during the day and then refreezing at night. This is something that many of us are used to.

But North France and Belgium during that winter was like nothing I had ever seen. When the temperatures dropped below zero, they would stay that way for weeks. It created great difficulties, little things that are easy to take for granted under anything close to normal conditions. We had a hard time with our water freezing up in our canteens. Since we were constantly under fire, we couldn't build a campfire to heat the water. Occasionally, we could use our Coleman lanterns. If we had a dugout, we would chop down a pine tree and use four-inch logs to make a roof. Our dugouts were about 4 feet by 8 feet and about 3 feet deep, usually on a rear-sloping hill. We

IF WE HAD A DUGOUT, WE WOULD CHOP DOWN A PINE TREE AND USE FOUR-INCH LOGS TO MAKE A ROOF. OUR DUGOUTS WERE ABOUT 4 FEET BY 8 FEET AND ABOUT 3 FEET DEEP, USUALLY ON A REAR-SLOPING HILL. WE WOULD BUILD UP THE SIDES WITH DIRT AND PLACE THE LOGS ON TOP TO COVER THE BRANCHES.

would build up the sides with dirt and place the logs on top to cover the branches. We'd pile on dirt and snow and make a half-door to the rear so that it was at least out of the wind. Only then could we break out our Colemans for heating, cooking, and melting snow.

We spent four hours in and four hours out of our foxholes, unless a German patrol attacked us. Sometimes, we could hear the Germans working or eating. If we detected activity, we would call in mortar fire. If we had an artillery spotter and a phone line intact, the spotter would call in an actual target. Our artillery was often busy firing on another request, so they could not fire or drop shells on our requested target.

Artillery was back about ten to fifteen miles from us. We discovered that we could get a priority shot by declaring "enemy in the open" or "visual." I was authorized to call artillery, using my ID, "222 at Havey." Using our map, I would give the grid coordinates and request WP (white phosphorous); this would serve as an "adjustment shell," or a visual marking of the area. If we had to call back for a second or third adjustment on the coordinates, the artillery coordinator would get worried and doubt our sightings. We would recheck our map information, but they usually knew where they were shooting. If our shell hit was on or near our target, we would get a call back that we were on target. They would fire for effect: four 105-mm or four 155-mm cannons. Everything would be aimed toward the target, and a box of fuselage consisting of four big shells would be fired, each about two to four times, depending upon shell supply. This creates a box of hell on your visual target, with high explosives and white phosphorous. The target box would be about 100 yards by 50 yards and about one-quarter of a football field. You could hear the shrapnel whine, see the shells explode and dirt fly, and watch as trees would break. We'd see smoke and a flash, and for a brief moment, we would forget how cold we were. We felt the power and pride of our division artillery.

> I WAS AUTHORIZED TO CALL ARTILLERY, USING MY ID, "222 AT HAVEY." USING OUR MAP, I WOULD GIVE THE GRID COORDINATES AND REQUEST WP (WHITE PHOSPHOROUS); THIS WOULD SERVE AS AN "ADJUSTMENT SHELL," OR A VISUAL MARKING OF THE AREA.

But the moment would pass quickly, and we would be back to our miserable, frozen reality. Our artillery support units were HQ 42nd Division Artillery, 232 Field Artillery, 393 Field Artillery, 402 Field Artillery, and 542 Field Artillery. All of us on the front line combat infantry loved our artillery support guys. Many believe the artillery guys are removed from the main line of resistance, but they are only back a few miles. They worked their butts off setting up, digging in, unloading equipment and ammo—basically, protecting us from the German attacks.

The Germans were busy sighting their own targets for counter battery fire. They were also setting up and digging in, creating their own foxholes. Our guys were the best, though. They tied phones into the battalion switchboard and snuggled up against the main line of resistance. They were ready to fire upon called targets and could pick a spot to shoot into the woods, which wasn't easy to find in a 360-degree position. They had to be prepared for MLR (main line of resistance; basically, the front) overrun, in which case they would actually become the infantry. This was all done in a defensive situation, but when we were attacking and moving forward (to say nothing of a retreat), they were setting up at each position and advancing two or three times daily or nightly.

This was the name of the game; we were attacking troops. We always needed them, and it was a matter of life and death. And all of this against that backdrop of miserable, biting cold.

There is the account of the famous withdrawal of the 42nd, at darkness on January 20, 1945. The weather conditions could not have been worse. The temperature was well below 20, and it was snowing heavily. But worst of all, the roads were covered with ice. Those roads were so bad that it was difficult for a man to walk more than a few yards without falling down. Even when proceeding slowly, trucks and tanks and artillery pieces would start to slide and end up with a crash in a ditch, or plunge over a bridge into a stream or ravine. It was hellacious trying to move through that stuff.

On top of it all, the men were tired from days and nights of almost constant moving and fighting—and they were hating that they were withdrawing.

There wasn't much talk as the men moved back. There was a curse now and then as a man slipped and fell, but he would pick himself up and trudge on.

"I'll bet I fell ten times a mile," one soldier declared later in a comment given for the official *42nd Rainbow Infantry Division: World War II History* record.[2]

The roads were lined with traffic, and although it would have been an excellent opportunity for the Germans to attack, the late-January withdrawal apparently took them by surprise. A few times their patrols contacted the rear guard, but they made no effort to advance.3

These bitter conditions were the curse of the winter of 1945.

On a few occasions during the snowy winter, we had to pass through areas in front of us that had been blasted by our own artillery, most likely high explosive shells or white phosphorous. The areas would still be smoking, and we'd come upon dead Germans who had seen, firsthand, the power of our artillery. Their dead bodies were frozen stiff, and the corpses were destined to remain there until spring, when the ground melted enough to dig fresh graves. Our gravediggers were too busy to worry about Germans, but we saw mounds of Krauts piled up after the Battle of the Bulge, so someone was handling them.

Thousands of our brave troops gave their lives and never came home. All these years later, that bothers me more than anything.

HEADQUARTERS
42D (RAINBOW) INFANTRY DIVISION

Office of the Commanding General

To the Men of the Rainbow Division:

This history of the Rainbow is a record of the accomplishments of every man who served in the Division. It is the story of his contribution to the safety and security of the people of his country and of the world.

It is a history made possible not by individual achievement, but by the combined effort of all. It is natural in such a history as this that the action of the front line soldier is emphasized. While he deserves every bit of credit that it is possible to give him, he realizes that he was able to fight and win only because he was a member of a great fighting team in which thousands of men united to defeat the enemy.

This, then, is a history of the combat infantry, of the artillery, the reconnaissance troop, the medical and engineer battalions, the signal, ordnance and quartermaster companies and of the division headquarters personnel.

It is the story of the Rainbow, and I am proud to have commanded its men in combat. I thank you for making this history possible—for a job well and bravely done.

Sincerely yours,

HARRY J. COLLINS
Major General, U. S. Army,
Commanding

The Rainbow Division endured hell to stop the Germans' invasion during the Battle of the Bitche Bulge—which came after the more famously known Battle of the Bulge. (Bitche is a city in northern France.) After the battle of the Bitche Bulge, we then to begin our own advance. This was a bulletin from Major General Harry J. Collins when the official record, or history, of the Rainbow was published. Collins wrote: "It is a history made possible not by individual achievement, but by the combined effort of all. . . . [This was] a great fighting team in which thousands of men united to defeat the enemy."

WINGEN-SUR-MODER BATTLE

Wingen-sur-Moder means the village of Wingen on the Moder River; this is in northeastern France, nestled in the Voggs Mountains . . .

Our company was ordered to redeploy west and withdraw back to several small towns destroyed by bombs. Captain George Waters took me in his Jeep to recon the route—to head out, scout, and see what the enemy is doing or where the enemy is. Still, that weather was raging. The roads were extremely icy and slick. Waters told me I was to lead the whole company of 250 men—all the guns, 57-mm anti-tank, trucks, and platoon officers—along the route of withdrawal. Wally, his driver, had night blindness and expected me to do his job as well. The officers—Mac, Fielding, Jack Westbrook, Lt. Davis, and Captain Waters—all had some duty at headquarters, leaving me in charge.

The heavy snow started about 4:30 PM, not that long before dark. It wasn't about to let up.

We pulled out in line about 6:30 PM. By now, it was dark and snowing even harder. From Soultz-sous-Foréts, France, we had about 25 miles ahead of us, moving along at the pace of 20 miles per hour. We came across a river, where literally hundreds of French refugees—old men, women, and children—were crossing the frigid, cold waters, fleeing the Germans, carrying what they could in carts and baby carriages. The refugees were fleeing, but also wanted to be with the U.S. Army for protection. There was just this problem: we were going in the opposite direction. The snow fell at unbelievable rates as we traveled in open Jeeps and trucks in temperatures in the teens. We sat in silence as we watched all those people fleeing for their lives. Even our motors were muffled. The entire scene was just surreal.

We didn't arrive at our first assigned village until long after midnight. Each platoon was given a small town to set up as MLR (main line of resistance). We were tasked with arranging fields of fire for our anti-tank guns. To this day, I still have some of those military maps.

Once we had our usual menu of cold water and crackers, we weren't permitted to smoke. It's what we called Silence and Sight. Anything that could be heard, seen, or even smelled was prohibited so that we would not give our location away. We had to dig holes and stay in position. We would shiver for hours. At least when we were digging, we stayed warm. We'd even break a sweat inside our dirty underwear! When we would stop digging and get into our holes for the night, all that sweat would then

I REMEMBER WIGGLING MY TOES TO KEEP MY FEET FROM FREEZING AND PUTTING MY HANDS IN MY ARMPITS IN HOPES OF KEEPING ALL MY FINGERS.

begin to reverse process and cool, then even start to freeze. We'd shiver something fierce. I remember wiggling my toes to keep my feet from freezing and putting my hands in my armpits in hopes of keeping all my fingers. Damn, it was so unbelievably cold. While in our holes, we would check our ammo, rifles, and grenades. Then we'd call it a night. We'd take turns being on watch, everyone basically waiting for daylight and what was to come.

The not knowing what was ahead kind of made dying not seem like the worst of things. It was the insane uncertainty—and cold—that messed with your mind. We all knew we could die at any point, and the war wouldn't miss us. By daylight, we were close to Wingen-sur-Moder, this cold, deserted town located in the midst of these hills. We strung out our line and occupied part of the destroyed houses. We used what we called an "in and out" system. We would stay in the holes for four hours, then in the house for four hours; this at least got us out of the wind and zero temperatures for a while.

In the house, we lit up our Coleman lantern and stoves to make some hot coffee. It might as well have been the Waldorf Hotel in New York! That coffee tasted so good, like nothing we'd ever drank before. Hell, we even had an outhouse with an ice-cold seat. The wind would whip up at your bare ass, but at least it was better than taking a crap outside. But oh, the process was miserable! First, we'd have to remove our cartridge belt, then move our grenades out of the way so we didn't blow ourselves up! Next, we'd pull off our bandolier that had 300 rounds of 30-mm ammunition, along with our overcoats. We could *then* unzip and pull down our shorts—all in frigid cold temps with wind. Having a cold seat to hop on was a luxury, to be honest. Each of us had toilet paper in our K rations, which was a good thing. Of course, you'd have to put yourself completely back together again after you went.

FEBRUARY 1945

Wingen saw some of the most intense house-to-house fighting of the entire Alsatian area. This was my experience as part of one of those battles.

The second morning of our stay at the "Waldorf," German artillery and mortar fire started. Fire was dropping in and around our positions. We were combat-wise and knew it was observed and visually directed fire. The house we were in had a tall deck with a red tile roof. We felt fairly safe keeping away from the windows, but all of a sudden, a machine gun fired up and down the street in front of us. I had a good line of sight up the road and saw an eighteen-man German combat patrol coming our way. Some of them were in white camouflage coats with white helmets. The mortar fire stopped, and we took our positions in the house. Hickey, from Chicago, was in the back kitchen covering the back door while Mouigaw, from Oregon, was up in the attic to snipe from the roof. Bob Crews was up the stairs and near the front windows. He only had a 45-caliber Colt pistol. Don't ask me why. I carried a 30-caliber carbine, two clips taped back to back.

I was up the stairs near the landing, facing the front door and dining room when the lead German patrol passed in front. Mouigaw opened up, killing him. Crews was firing out the upstairs window like a wild west cowboy! I heard a Kraut shot, and Crews fell back from the window with blood streaming out of his forehead. To this day, whenever I see a stream, I still think of Crews and how he got shot. What a cold, dirty way to go, especially considering that he'd eventually get wrapped up in a cheap mattress cover. That visual remains with me to this day. Crews fell straight back, dead, without another sound or movement.

> TO THIS DAY, WHENEVER I SEE A STREAM, I STILL THINK OF CREWS AND HOW HE GOT SHOT.

I saw the front door open about a foot, and a grenade blew the door wide open. A German rushed in with another behind him. The first headed toward me on the stairs, but he was looking down the hall, so he never saw me. I shot him point blank in the head. He fell back and to his right. The second German looked up and started to raise his rifle, but I got a shot off first. I hit him in the center of his body. He was blown halfway out the door, but his legs were still inside.

I heard Hickey in the kitchen yelling, "Don't shoot, don't shoot!" and then all was quiet. I then heard a machine gun firing from under the front kitchen window. I unclipped a grenade from my belt strap and went down the stairs about ten steps. I saw the German I had shot in the head. The entire left side of his head was gone, but he still had a bit of life in him. It's one of the oddities of war: with half of his head gone, his right eye followed me as I stepped around him to make my way to the front window. I still heard bursts of gunfire along with German words being spoken. I didn't want to create noise by shooting, so I pulled the pin on my grenade and tossed the handle. Looking out the window, I had seen the German machine gun set up on the porch. I put the grenade right on top of the machine gun—there were three guys on the porch—and slipped back. I

BIRNEY T. "CHICK" HAVEY

heard a voice yell "Grenade!"—like: "Gre-NAH-dee," in German—and it blew. That took care of the firing, killing one German on the porch and wounding the two others.

One of the next things I remember is seeing our medic, in his white cover blouse with red cross, treating both Germans and our man, Barney, with head bandages. About ten minutes later, two of our Sherman tanks came rolling into town, firing machine guns up the road. Those tankers finished off the battle and made the difference. The lead tank had run over one of the white-camouflaged Germans, length-wise. The guy was flat as a pancake, with tread marks and blood juice squirting out each side.

I was still pissed as I walked by, smelling fresh blood once again. Two dead, two wounded, and one missing. The Battle of Wingen-sur-Moder. I was lucky to be alive, but we did our jobs and held the line.

* * * *

In the hell of war, it's only much later that you can assess your thoughts, so I was pretty unemotional, even after the house battle. We were kind of used it, so I tried to be as unemotional as I could. We went out and hollered at those tankers, thanking them. They had made the difference. They saved our butts. And we just left from there and rejoined our company.

* * * * *

We received the Presidential Unit Citation for our work along the MLR in the Alsace. It's hard not to feel damned proud. The citation reads, in part:

**Presidential Unit Citation to the 222nd Infantry Regiment
For Extraordinary Heroism in Military Operations Against
an Armed Enemy
24 January 1945 to 25 January 1945**

*The 222nd Infantry Regiment is cited for extraordinary and outstanding performance of duty in action against the enemy on 24 and 25 January 1945, in the Bois D'Ohlungen, and the vicinity of Schweighausen and Neuborg, France. On the night of 24 January 1945, the 222nd . . . under strength by half a Battalion of riflemen, yet necessarily extended over a 7,500-yard front, was attacked by five regiments from the 7th Parachute, 25th Panzer, and 47th German VG Divisions which were supported by heavy artillery. Ordered to hold at all costs, the Regiment withstood the enemy's desperate bid to break the Seventh Army Moder River Line. Fighting back from ice-filled foxholes, the outnumbered defenders fought off wave after wave of enemy attacking all along the Regiment's front and infiltrating into friendly positions, well behind the Main Line of Resistance. Wild fighting raged throughout the night and well into the next day as the fanatical attackers sought to break out into open country, but every measure was met by determined counterattacks. On the night of the 25th, the frustrated enemy fell back to his original line, leaving the ground littered with enemy dead. Despite the loss of 237 officers and men, the 222nd Infantry Regiment held its position, exacting a heavy toll of men and equipment from the enemy. The courage and devotion to duty shown by the members of the 222nd . . . in smashing one of the enemy's principal strategic efforts to reconquer Alsace, are worthy of emulation and ex*emplify the highest traditions of the Army of the United States.

PRISONER PATROL

The 222nd Regiment was back up on the MLR (main line of resistance) around Wingen-sur-Moder in the Vosges Mountains. The weather report was predicting wet conditions with light, cold snow. It was still very cold, even in late February. The temperature at night was going to get down into the teens. We felt like we would never get out of those damn hills. I don't know what our commander did to General Eisenhower to piss him off, but we were stuck. Our company was strung out over a mile on the front lines in those hills. Foxholes were spaced about fifty yards

IN THAT HEAVY, WOODED FOREST, THE GERMANS COULD HAVE RUN THEIR ENTIRE ARMY THROUGH OUR SPREAD-OUT LINE.

apart, and the line—and the holes—were leaky, to say the least. In that heavy, wooded forest, the Germans could have run their entire army through our spread-out line.

We were dug in those foxholes and bunker stations. Line patrol was set up with a phone line intact. We would run four-man patrols in and among our own lines to maintain contact. The Germans were supposed to be a crack SS outfit, now re-fitted from the Battle of the Bulge and fully capable of resist-ing. Apparently, they were part of a Norway SS unit after Hitler captured Norway. This Norwegian army consisted of youths who were convinced they were the true Aryan race and would, therefore, rule the world. These Norwegians had special black uniforms and caps, and they thought they were something spe-cial. I happen to have insights into their activity, and I got to share all that with the people who lived in the house where we battled, in Wingen-sur-Moder, when I visited there sixty-nine years later, in 2014.

Wingen was a special place of killing during two or three sep-arate battles; this is why Mrs. Linda Bergmann, who lives there today, and welcomed us in for dinner in 2013, had pictures of the Norway SS troops in her museum. Yes, a museum. An al-cove area is set up as a small museum of sorts, with all sorts of relics, helmets and things like that. It is a nice residence—right there at 7 Rue de Zittersheim, Wingen-sur-Moder, France—and they have turned the property back into a working motorcycle shop. We joined them for dinner and tea. She has markers set up where the men fell during that house battle. Seven of them; she has seven markers in and around the house where the bod-ies fell. That house will always be an amazing place in my mem-ory. It's where I easily could have died; but the Germans—and our guy Crews—fell instead. In my visit back in 2013, we were also able to see some of the emplacements where German ma-chine gun nests were set up, out back. Still there, seven decades later, those emplacements.

Some of the survivors from Norway visited her after the war, Mrs. Bergmann said. That house is where I earned my Silver Star decoration. Needless to say, I did not have all the information that I have now during my time on this front!

* * * *

But back to late February: things were relatively quiet, except when opposing patrols would run into each other. A firefight would break out with mortar fire, and then we would be busy. Stretches would go by with some killed, others wounded—and medics and the injured would weave through those trees on their way back to the hospital. At night, they would pass back through our lines with two-man hand carriers. Most firing would be quiet while both sides focused on the dirty work needed to help the medics.

Word came down from G2—that was the designation for our division's intelligence—that the general needed more information about the enemy facing us and behind them. He wanted to know if a buildup for an attack was occurring. The best way to get that information was by taking prisoners from enemy troops. That way, Division Intel could put the squeeze on the prisoner and find out if he knew anything.

Well, General Collins, whom we called Hollywood Harry, sent an order down for our regimental commanders to offer a special prize for enemy captures: a three-day pass to Paris. So each company sent out patrols looking for prisoners; the goal was to bring back one man per trip. One evening, about eight of us were gathered around our Coleman stove getting ready to eat when the wind out of the north started blowing cold, dry snow. Lieutenant McEndorfer came over looking for volunteers for that night's patrol. Up until now, we hadn't heard about the prize for a successful capture. He informed us about the pass to Paris. Renick, from Illinois, spoke up right away. I kind of mulled it over; it didn't take me too long to figure a trip to Paris would be pretty good. The third volunteer was King, and he was half nuts. Three men were all we wanted for this kind of mission, and all three of us were experienced. This was not our first ballgame.

THREE MEN WERE ALL WE WANTED FOR THIS KIND OF MISSION, AND ALL THREE OF US WERE EXPERIENCED. THIS WAS NOT OUR FIRST BALLGAME.

We were to leave our lines about midnight; the thinking was the Germans would be sleeping and less alert, especially in light of the new-fallen snow. Vision was limited, and the snow on the trees made everything seem very quiet. We were promised some outgoing 81-mm cover fire early on for the patrol. We stripped down to field jackets, cartridge belts, one bandolier of 30-cal, two frag grenades, and one white phosphorous grenade each. We had our knives, M-1 rifles, and helmets. No canteens. Believe it or not, you could pick up sound better with that bell-shape helmet. The three of us was all we had; this was our kidnap patrol.

I don't remember what our password was, but we sure as hell knew it then.

Our front line listening post was notified of our in-and-out mission and that we'd be coming and going. Going out on patrol is easy, but finding your way back without getting shot is an entirely different matter. Sometimes, we would hang a rag in a tree limb, but we still had to remember our way back in the dark. Talk about bird dogs! You have to develop instincts and smarts if you want to survive. However, you are pretty confident that you aren't going to make it home. A vicious, wicked cycle. It was what it was.

King was a big blond guy. He was a strong kid and an auto mechanic back in St. Louis before the war. We were all something different before this hell. King survived the war, but was killed in 1948 in St. Louis trying to help a motorist change a tire. How's that for irony? I can still see the smile on his face, 70 years later.

* * * *

Renick was in his first year of college in Champagne, Illinois. After we first broke into Germany, he and I had a routine of searching each house in the town. As we advanced, taking what we wanted—which was how it was in war—our prizes became gold, silver watches, cameras, and Luger and P38 pistols. We left the German money because it was worthless to us, but we saw plenty of it. Our gas masks strapped over our shoulders made a mighty fine carrying case for trade and barter.

A story about Renick from a different time in the war: He had come to me and asked me to teach him how to loot. I gave him a few pointers, like looking under coal piles, floorboards, that sort of thing. He needed to look in places where people would normally hide stuff. Remember, all this was going on while we were still being shot at. Our chances of getting blown up were high, and the ways to get killed were limitless.

OUR CHANCES OF GETTING BLOWN UP WERE HIGH, AND THE WAYS TO GET KILLED WERE LIMITLESS.

Our slogan became: "Out of a squad of twelve men, two men are shootin' and ten men are lootin.'" Our attitude was that we didn't start this war, and since we were brought all this way, we would take what we could. They certainly didn't show us any mercy.

Three days after teaching Renick the ropes of looting, we were moving through a partly captured town. We were street fighting, clearing out a row of flats, using our snipers on the highest roofs. I kicked down a dwelling door and searched the place. I heard a lot of noise and yelling out back. Lo and behold, my student looter had two Germans—civilians—begging for their lives. Renick had his rifle to their heads was making them dig their own graves. He found a camera lens cover in the house, and they would not give it up. They didn't seem to know where the camera was, but it was hard to tell exactly what was going on since neither party spoke the other's language! Renick never found that camera, and he didn't shoot the Germans; we turned them over to the division. An amazing scene. War made you do crazy things.

> LO AND BEHOLD, MY STUDENT LOOTER HAD TWO GERMANS— CIVILIANS—BEGGING FOR THEIR LIVES. RENICK HAD HIS RIFLE TO THEIR HEADS WAS MAKING THEM DIG THEIR OWN GRAVES.

* * * *

So, as I mentioned, our patrol was scheduled to leave at midnight. General Collins was looking for prisoners to obtain vital information. We'd beat it out of them, is what we'd do, just like they beat it out of us. This was war. About midnight, we crept out to our line patrol listening post to get any information they might have on enemy activity. Anything they could tell us about gun bursts, mortar firing, the tinkling sounds of chow pans, chatter—anything like that might help us locate the enemy line. We would also speak with their relief team because they most likely wouldn't be on the line when we returned. They did four hours on and four hours off.

After getting what we needed, we slipped out to begin our mission. We worked our way through draws and valleys and through the German lines. At this point, our noses took over. The wind had slowed down, and we were like bird dogs. We could smell their dugouts, with logs covering them up, some of them with flap-covered doorways. But I'll tell you that our scent detection was mainly the German soldiers' Turkish tobacco cigarette smell; any close-combat GI will know what I mean. That's the scent we picked up when we really knew we were close.

We also noticed all kinds of footprints in the snow around us. I sneaked up to one of the doorways with a white phos grenade ready. I popped it and opened the flap and then dropped it in. I moved to the side of the dugout, ready to knock somebody in the head with my rifle.

The grenade went off with a *woosh!* . . . *bang!* . . . and out the Germans came, yelling as they were being burned. Sure enough, I ended up hitting one over the head—who wasn't burning—and I pulled his body by the foot down to the slope where King and Renick were waiting. We gagged him with a first aid pack and tied his hands behind his back. My belt was around his neck so we could control him. We took turns dragging him the next one hundred yards. He started coming to, but was in a daze.

We got him on his feet and started back, but those damn Germans never gave up. The prisoner started fighting back, and I beat the bastard. We forced him to keep moving and came to a wire fence. We threw him over like a sack of coal. I saw the hill silhouette and knew we were on the right track to get back. Dawn was starting to break, and there was a low frost cloud on the ground. We arrived at our line patrol and delivered the prisoner to our platoon HQ, where he would be interrogated. It turned out that this particular outfit had not been previously identified on our front. This meant that our general wanted more information from additional prisoners. We ducked out of that one, however. Don't ask me how.

* * * *

We did earn a trip to Paris. The only problem was only one of us could go. Captain Waters had us draw straws to see who would get to take the trip. Lieutenant McEndorfer held two long and one short straw for us to pick from. I went first and got a long straw. Renick went next and got the winning short straw, and thus the trip to Paris. Oh well, C'est la vie, as the French say. That's life.

> WHAT WE DID WASN'T ANYTHING EXCEPTIONAL, BECAUSE HUNDREDS OF GUYS WERE JUST AS BRAVE, DOING THE SAME MISSIONS AND PATROLS UP AND DOWN SOME THREE HUNDRED MILES OF FRONT LINES.

Looking back, though, I do wish I would have chosen second.

What we did wasn't anything exceptional, because hundreds of guys were just as brave, doing the same missions and patrols up and down some three hundred miles of front lines. I just happen to still be living and able to share my story. I'm grateful for the memory to do so, and I hope you know that because of what we all did, you are able to walk free today.

May none of us ever forget.

Medics

In our basic training we learned to use bandage packs that we carried on our belts. The packs contained a long piece of gauze with a built-in pad sealed and sterile, along with a small package of sulfa dusting powder; the gauze was long enough to make an arm sling.

When I was wounded in battle, through my right hand, I used my bandage; one of the guys tied it on. I had a little sulfa left for my right arm. "Shorty," our medic, was not in the area, so I walked back to the battalion aid station and got a ride back to the field hospital from there.

Shorty was a well-liked guy; he had exposed himself to danger many times. I cannot remember his real name and he is not part of our platoon roster, so I am still searching for his name to this day, but there doesn't seem to be anyone left to ask. (Maybe someone reading this book will know of Shorty and can provide me the information.) He wore that white smock with the red cross front and back, the white circle and cross on his helmet, and carried his medical bag over his shoulder in addition to his blanket roll and tent half.

During the battle at Wingen-sur-Moder, Shorty was out in the street, Barney was dead, and the bullets were flying. Monaghan laughed about this afterward as he had an exceptional view. He shot one German in the ass who was hiding behind a tree across the street. That German pulled in his ass and then stuck out his head, and then Monaghan shot him in the head. Shorty was at work through all of this, putting dressings on our guys who had been shot; all the while the bullets were flying from both the Germans and our platoon out on those snow-covered streets of Wingen.

* * * *

Going back to Camp Gruber in Oklahoma, in the fall of 1944, before the 42nd shipped to Europe, one of the final tests for the infantry was a 25-mile hike that had to be completed by the company in six hours. Shorty had to tag along with us during that final hike to pop—and then care for— various foot blisters. So Shorty had been with us, and we knew his dedication.

It wasn't unusual for some of the weaker men to fall over and out of line during a march. Shorty would be on the job to check them out and determine whether they needed an ambulance. During our ten-minute break each hour—and they stuck to that schedule rigidly—Shorty would have long lines of troops to see to treat their foot blisters with his needle, letting the fluid out of a blister, and generally helping us all to continue the 25-mile test march. When we were done, our company would get a "well done," which meant we were deemed in good shape and ready to go off to war—to get killed or wounded. But I can tell you that conditioning did save lives, no question about that.

* * * *

Unless you have been there, one cannot begin to imagine the dirty conditions of a battlefield: no hot water, no sterile rubber gloves, no one has bathed for thirty to sixty days, your hands are covered brown with dirt, and we were lucky to have drinking water, let alone water to wash ourselves. There were no sterile soaps.

A piercing wound—like that which went through my hand—carried bits of clothing and dirt in with it, let alone the dirt on the projectile. It's hard to see how they ever cleaned up a wound with those conditions, but our medics were second to none.

Conditions would be much better at the field hospitals, where you could get a bath and white sheets. That's where I spent eight days healing my hand, but I kept pestering the doctor to let me go back to my company. I did not want to be assigned to the "repo depot" (replacement troops depot) where I would never make it back to my outfit and friends. So after convincing a Doctor Flores that I was without fever and well, he discharged me after morning rounds. I took my stuff in a pillowcase and started my way back, hitching rides.

I got back to division headquarters, then regimental HQ, to battalion, and finally to our company. That's a hard road to cover, as we were on the move. By the time I got back I had scrounged up a pack, an M-1 rifle, two blankets, and a cartridge belt. The supply sergeant at our company, a Sergeant Adkins, had kept my knife, helmet, and loot bag intact for me. And they still carried my barracks bag with my uniform and some personal stuff, so I was back in business. It had been easy to hitchhike a ride back, as my hand was still bandaged. The guys were all glad to have me back, especially Captain Waters.

* * * *

My folks back home in St. Louis received their war department telegram:

Your son, Private Birney T. Havey Jr., was wounded in action, in Northern France, on March 1, 1945. Your country and the President of the United States of America express their gratitude for your sacrifice.

(Signed) The Secretary of War

It is hard to imagine what my mother and family thought on receiving that communication from a messenger on his bicycle. No other information was given beyond that: nothing about the battle, the wound, and, of course, nothing about my condition or prognosis.

My mother saved every letter from me over my four years in the army. I have them to this day, kept in her little box tied up with some seventy-year-old string; her little knots are still holding up! One letter stands out. It was written on March 1, the very morning of the day I would be wounded.

* * * *

Now, of course, we hardly ever knew what day of the week it was, let alone the date. We seemed to be pretty up on the months, however, as we knew that spring was coming and that it was getting warmer each day. But I can tell you it was still freezing at night after sunset.

Shorty would have in his medical bag four 1,000-liter bottles of I.V. plasma. This is sort of a wonder drug for the bleeding and wounded. I can't tell you how many times I would see Shorty holding up that plasma bottle or having a helper hold up the bottle for him while he worked on the wounded soldier. You can imagine how brutal cold it would have been in the winter-time, and Shorty would try to keep that plasma warm by holding it against his body.

Shorty would also carry morphine serrets. I have never heard of anyone abusing these painkillers; no wounded, unless he was surely dying, could tolerate more than two serrets of morphine, because of the shock of getting the drug in the winter at 10 to 20 degrees below zero. We lost plenty of men to the shock and cold; if it had been warm, they would have had a better chance of living.

We had some comfort in knowing that the Germans were cold too. I think Shorty and his assistant, who I never really knew, were assigned to our company from our battalion aid station. I know their medical supplies came up by Jeep, and they removed wounded and the dead back by Jeep. We saw very few ambulances unless we were on the move forward.

The best I can do is pen this short tribute to Shorty and the hundreds of medics and their assistants who worked tirelessly, as he did. I very much wish I could find his real name. The men of the Rainbow Division, like myself, owed him—and them—so much.

THE PURPLE HEART

The Badge of Military Merit, frequently called the Purple Heart, was created by General George Washington on August 7, 1782. The Badge, the figure of a heart in purple cloth of silk edged with narrow lace or binding, was awarded in recognition of unusual gallantry, extraordinary fidelity, and essential service. Only three awards of the badge were originally recorded. After the Revolutionary War, the decoration went into disuse, although it was never abolished.

The Purple Heart was revived by order of President Herbert Hoover on February 22, 1932, as a bronze and enamel decoration in the form of a purple heart, bearing the likeness and coat of arms of General Washington. The decoration was awarded in recognition of singularly meritorious acts of extraordinary fidelity or essential service. Wounds received in action against an enemy of the United States were considered as resulting from such acts.

* * * *

It was after the battle in Wingen-sur-Moder that I was shot through the right hand. The piercing bullet hit my rifle and knocked the rifle stock off, and part of the shrapnel went into my left arm.

I saw my blood go into the soil and I thought . . . I remember thinking, *Here goes some more blood into the ground of France.*

Now, for a moment, allow me to fast forward sixty-eight years later, just a year or two back, when I cut my hand while at my daughter's, working in her yard. I remember seeing blood drip out of my hand into the ground. Standing there, I was suddenly transported back to France in Winter 1945. Talk about bringing back memories, or déjà vu. All I could think of was being back in France.

* * * *

The Purple Heart is displayed at the Normandy American Military Cemetery as a "Perpetual Symbol of the Profound Gratitude of a Bereaved Nation for the Devotion and Sacrifice of the Heroes who are Commemorated Here."

* * * *

I am listed on a sheet—marked "Restricted"—that I still have to this day, dated 23 April 1945—under the office of "Headquarters 42d Infantry Division," General Orders. Seventy-five men are listed, and I am the thirteenth down the list. On the sheet, I underlined a couple of buddies I knew who also received the Purple Heart.

AWARD OF PURPLE HEART

Under the provisions of Army Regulations 600-45, as amended, the Purple Heart is awarded to the following for wounds received in action against the enemy:

BIRNEY T. HAVEY, 17 075 652, Private First Class, Infantry, Anti-tank Company, 222d Infantry Regiment, France, 1 March 1945. Entered military service from St. Louis, Missouri.

My buddies listed are **Earl E. Fleisher**, also 222d Anti-tank, Allentown, Pa., wounded 25 January 1945; and **Archie R. Monaghan**, also 222d Anti-tank, Bellingham, Wash., wounded 26 January 1945.

It is signed:

By command of Major General COLLINS.

THE SIEGFRIED
LINE

The Siegfried line was a connection of underground forts strung from the Swiss border to the Belgium border on the western-southern German border, facing France. It was built in the 1930s when Hitler was gaining power over the German government and trashing the 1918 Allies and German Geneva surrender treaty of Versailles. The rolling countryside of the border between France and Germany was farmland. Original forts at France's Maginot Line were built as a sort of countermeasure to the Siegfried as France faced Germany. After World War I, U.S. newspapers printed a running account of both projects—Siegfried and Maginot—for years, along with photos, especially of the French forts.

Hitler's buildings were more or less a secret, as was his violation of Germany's treaty obligations. Little did I, a boy growing up in St. Louis, know at the time that these occasional newspaper accounts were a foretelling of future events that would ultimately involve me on the Siegfried Line, which was built from 1936 to 1940.

St. Louis had multiple newspapers, such as the *Morning St. Louis, Globe Democrat,* and *Evening St. Louis Post,* along with three or four radio stations: KWK, KSD, and KMOX, as I recall them. (Each newspaper was delivered to your door by a teenaged boy running his own business. The paper cost was two cents, until they raised it to three cents, which is a 50 percent increase! Each delivery boy was assigned his routes and was responsible for not only delivering the papers but also collecting payments.) When something big happened, "Extras" were printed to highlight the sensational event. The newsboys would come through the neighborhood streets shouting, "Extra, extra! Hitler marches into the Alsace Lorraine!" or "German troops cross the Rhine!" People would run out of their homes to buy these extra papers. This is about the time when I learned of Hitler's secret construction of the Siegfried Line of forts. The purpose of the Siegfried was originally to protect Germany's left flank from France, if and when they attacked through Belgium. The question I had was, "Where were the people running France and England at that time in history?" Even as a boy growing up, I could see the problem.

Little did I know that the Siegfried was merging to a point

by Ludwigswinkle (Germany) and Alsace (France) on the German border in 1945. Some sixty-nine years later, I write these stories from memory of my direct experience. I did not conduct research or read books to learn about these stories because I actually *lived* them. I have been quite amazed at my long-term memory and recall, at the age of 93, these events in history well. The events of that era were exceptional to say the least. (So I ask you to realize that my account is meant to not be official history, but a soldier's recounting of an amazing time.)

CUTTING THROUGH THE HIGHWAY

In some cases, dates are difficult to pinpoint. When we were in battle, we were on the move. As I have said, in the infantry, you hardly know what month it was, let alone the exact date. Days and weeks were of no consequence. All we knew was that each day was more of the same misery and danger. I did obtain a military reference of our actual company's daily log. This describes the battles with dates, towns, and even weather forecasts. (This book is *The Story of the Rainbow, 42nd Rainbow Infantry Division: World War II History*, Army and Navy Publishing Company. A full reference to this gem of history is in my notes at the end of this book, for those who are interested in learning more. The details of the heart of the first push through that line, March 15-

WE WERE ON FOOT THROUGH THE HARDT MOUNTAINS, TAKING THE OFFENSIVE POSITION. WE WERE ABOUT HALF-STARVED, CLIMBING UP AND DOWN THE MOUNTAINS, LOSING MEN LEFT AND RIGHT. OLD MISSOURI-TYPE MULES WERE CARRYING OUT THE WOUNDED ON SIDE STRETCHERS.

17, into the Hardt Mountains, are given in fascinating detail.) Otherwise, my stories are to the best of my recollection, as I lived them.

We were on foot through the Hardt mountains, taking the offensive position. We were about half-starved, climbing up and down the mountains, losing men left and right. Old Missouri-type mules were carrying out the wounded on side stretchers. One side might carry a dead soldier while the other side would have a wounded man, lying there bleeding. We had these pack mules attached to our regiment to pack out the wounded and dead, of which we had plenty, and we kept those old mules busy. They carried their own feed, which was better than what we were eating at the time! In one attack to cut through a highway—the highway ran between Haguenau and a town called Bitche—we were given one day's ration, or a K ration, which included breakfast, lunch, dinner, and a D Ration bar. This all weighed about three pounds. Our biggest need was to carry ammunition: bazooka, mortar, and 30-caliber weapons. Our orders were to punch through German front lines and then surround them, which we did. We kept moving forward as the Germans pounded the tall forest trees with artillery and shells that screamed as they came in.

Typical K rations for breakfast were light-brown water and eggs and pork that came out of a wax-covered box. We were each given three cigarettes, some matches, and crackers. Our pack included a small roll of toilet paper, one cup of Nescafé, some sugar, and cream. Lunch was about the same, except we got a can of Velveeta cheese and a fig-raisin bar as big as your thumb, wrapped in cellophane. The third meal box, or dinner, was the same, with the addition of a pork hash.

The third day of climbing up and down that damned mountain caused us to become weak to the point where we were physically lifting our legs with our hands and pulling ourselves up by our pants leg. We had no option but to keep going; we could not stop or go back.

Thankfully, we had enough water because of the fresh mountain streams. We were able to fill our canteens and do so often, and it was nice, clean stream water. I remember a point when a fellow soldier and I were filling up our canteens when, about a hundred yards upstream, we noticed two freshly killed Germans bleeding out in the water. We looked at one another and said, "Oh well," and kept refilling our canteens. We drank that water without a second thought to the dead bodies in the stream. We just didn't give a damn because we were glad to have the water. War was like that.

When I look back on this operation, I realize that, to be truthful, all we were doing was trying to find a better place to get ourselves killed. We suffered severe hunger pangs. On the eve before we reached our objective of cutting through that highway, we finally received some food. We stood around this full case of K Rations like a pack of wild dogs. To us, it looked like Thanksgiving dinner. We ate, dug in, and rested for the night.

The next morning, three German tanks on that highway cut loose on us, coming from the wooded hill and firing into our line. We all set records digging in so fast, and we forced the tanks to withdraw. I think they ran out of ammo, but they also couldn't move forward without infantry to protect them. We did better than I thought we would during that battle, to be honest. I'll never know, though, what really happened with those Germans.

On my first trip back to France since the war, in 2013, we passed that same spot on that highway. Time had changed the woods, and I could not find the battle spot. But the hills were the same, and the trees were still dark pines. That soft dirt always made for good digging of foxholes.

As we moved on, we started to get into some very deep crap.

Don't ask me why, but our 222nd Infantry Regiment was chosen by the 7th Army to lead the assault through the famous German Siegfried line of forts, this line we had all heard so much about. And trust me, whatever you have heard, you've only got about half of the story.

After moving up to the edge of the Siegfried Line—we hadn't yet penetrated it—about four of the guys were on a high bluff looking down on a big valley that had two lakes and a roadway running across our front. Watching our big, Long Tom artillery fire into a line across those lakes came with this excellent mountain view. The Long Tom shells were passing just over our dumb heads, sounding like trains whizzing by; the sound was that intense. God only knows how close they were, but it seemed they weren't above us more than a few feet. Those Long Toms could fire for a distance of about 25 miles. I think they were attached to our corps, as our division had only 155-mm Howitzers with a 15-mile range.

AS WE MOVED ON, WE STARTED TO GET INTO SOME VERY DEEP CRAP. DON'T ASK ME WHY, BUT OUR 222ND INFANTRY REGIMENT WAS CHOSEN BY THE 7TH ARMY TO LEAD THE ASSAULT THROUGH THE FAMOUS GERMAN SIEGFRIED LINE OF FORTS, THIS LINE WE HAD ALL HEARD SO MUCH ABOUT.

By mid-afternoon, we knew the real attack would jump off about midnight. The Long Toms were shooting up those German defenders. And I'm not sure how they did it since the Germans were in those three-foot-thick pillboxes.

The company runner, Vic, comes over and tells me and Captain Waters that we need to head over to the company HQ. "I am to lead you there," Vic said. Well, this Vic is the same guy who jumped out of our window during a grenade joke the month before. (This story is coming later in the book.) I was the company commander's bodyguard, and I knew something was up . . . big time. As I've mentioned, Captain Waters was from Rome, New York. (My mother and his wife were corresponding and had exchanged gifts for his baby daughter.)

Captain Waters and I had made a sworn deal after our first combat together in this great Battle of the Bulge. While in the task force at Linden, he called me in and said, "Havey, I know you are a good soldier. You are brave and smart. I want you to try your best to see to it that I get home. I want to see my wife and daughter in New York. For this, I will carry you on my roster as my orderly with almost all the benefits of an officer. At company HQ, you will remain a private first class, but all my platoon will know your real status." Well, as events unfolded, his trust in me grew to the point where I was able to speak on his behalf to company HQ. All company officers accepted this, and all went well—other than my short, ten-day stay in the hospital when I was wounded. After I got back, everyone was glad to see me. Frankly, all I did was follow orders and convey them well. That was our deal.

THE SIEGFRIED ATTACK: WATERS AND I PROBE THE LINE

Back to the Siegfried Line attack: the division commander, General Collins, wanted to know firsthand, that night, if those two bridges seen from the bluffs would be safe for Sherman tanks to cross during the attack. Our First Battalion of the 222nd Infantry had been the ones chosen to die there, so our Commanding Officer (CO) was not too busy as to follow the reinforcements. So General Collins wanted an experienced patrol to seek and report this information.

By this time, the Germans had awakened and had started shelling and firing. Captain Waters volunteered a two-man patrol to head into the Siegfried to check those two bridges for tank passage. About 9 PM, three hours before the jump-off of the main attack, Captain Waters and I led the whole Seventh Army into the much-talked-about, vaunted German Siegfried Line. This was the last place in the world any sane person would want to be. I looked over at Captain Waters, and he didn't have any grenades. He only had his 45-cal Colt army pistol. I told him what a fine mess we were in, as if I had to say anything. He was just kind of indifferent and resolved. I was leading about twenty yards ahead on the far bank along the road, watching out the best I could for mines in the dark. Some of our own machine guns were firing overhead, hitting the metal telephone poles, ricocheting and zinging off. I could tell by the rate of fire and sound that they were our machine guns. Suddenly, I caught a whiff of Germans. Anyone who has been in close combat and is still living can tell you what I mean. It was that Turkish tobacco smell I mentioned earlier; it was just something you were certain about when you came up on them.

> CAPTAIN WATERS AND I LED THE WHOLE SEVENTH ARMY INTO THE MUCH-TALKED-ABOUT, VAUNTED GERMAN SIEGFRIED LINE. THIS WAS THE LAST PLACE IN THE WORLD ANY SANE PERSON WOULD WANT TO BE.

I slid back to Captain Waters and told him I did not need him and his pistol. There was going to be a whole lot of shooting, and soon, and I didn't want him to get shot. I moved forward from there, my senses keen. I located the German listening post and its occupants. Not only could I smell them, I was right *on* them. I readied my grenade and shot the two sitting together facing me. I let the grenade go and ducked; the explosion and shrapnel flew everywhere. I received some return fire, but I located the source quickly. It was quite far away and was hitting in the lake to our left and behind.

I went back and got Captain Waters and said, "I think it's clear," and we slithered forward along the ditch to the first bridge, which was a strong little span over a deep valley stream. Waters was watching while I checked the first bridge for wires and mines. We could never be too careful. All was OK. I didn't find any mines, wires, or charges. We walked another hundred yards to the second bridge, and that felt like a really long way.

I kept Captain Waters behind me about thirty yards. Crossing that stream under the first bridge required going through waist-deep running water. The night was extremely frosty, but no matter; we pressed on and back up on the road by the ditch, where we found two dead American soldiers with helmets on and rifles in hand. I will probably never know how they died. We passed them and continued on to the second, larger bridge. There was no German listening post at this one. Captain Waters stayed back as I checked for wires and mines. All seemed good, and the bridge was made of strong steel. Having completed our mission, we needed to return to our line. That was another matter altogether.

'WHAT'S A FELLOW GOT TO DO TO GET SOME SLEEP AROUND HERE?'

It was after midnight by now, and the 222nd attack had jumped off. Here we were in no-man's-land between the German Siegfried and our own Seventh Army. Peachy. Just peachy. The two lead U.S. scouts were moving toward the deadly fire from the enemy. Fire was cutting over them and the lead elements of the First Platoon. One scout was about 50 yards in front of the other.

It was pitch black and past midnight. But we could see as if it was daylight because the skyline was a constant glow from thousands of distant shell bursts. The only real light we had in front of us was an occasional shell falling along the front. We let the first scout go past, and the second came up to us. We started whispering loudly, "222nd patrol!"; this was the password of the day. Passwords saved lives. Without them, guys got shot by their own people—sad fact, but true. You just didn't go around wandering in the middle of the night around a bunch of amped-up guys with weapons.

> WE STARTED WHISPERING LOUDLY, "222ND PATROL!"; THIS WAS THE PASSWORD OF THE DAY. PASSWORDS SAVED LIVES. WITHOUT THEM, GUYS GOT SHOT BY THEIR OWN PEOPLE—SAD FACT, BUT TRUE.

The scouts were startled, and I remember the looks on those brave faces. They were in a tough spot out there in no-man's-land in front of the vaunted Siegfried Line. The officer in charge came up to where he was instructed. All was clear up to the bridges and Captain Waters. We then headed back to report to regimental headquarters. Colonel Luongo and I branched off and went back to our company, where we were to move through the First Battalion and up the hill to set up a perimeter defense against German counterattacks. We saw the light of dawn by this point and got past the bridges and into those hills. We dug in and ate breakfast on the forward slope of the hills just past the bridges.

We were dug in about a hundred yards from a reinforced German concrete pillbox that was deserted. Apparently, the

Germans retreated across the Rhine River at Worms in an attempt to set up a flank. It was good news for us. I leaned back in my foxhole and took a nap. We had been up all night.

I was awakened by a three-quarter-ton truck pulling up close to my hole. It was a detail of combat engineers carrying a full case of quarter-pound blocks of TNT explosives into the back steel door of the German pillbox. They were setting up an electric fuse system, and soon they were yelling "Fire in the hole!" as they set off the cases of TNT. Well, it burned hot with a lot of smoke coming out the back door of the pillbox. It didn't damage that sturdy pillbox whatsoever, though. These were the orders for those engineers: to destroy that box so the Germans couldn't reoccupy it in the event they would win back our captured territory. About an hour later, here came a two-and-a-half-ton truck loaded with about thirty cases of TNT. *What does a fellow have to do to get some sleep around here?*, I thought. With all of that TNT, it took them about an hour to unload it into the pillbox. They came over to warn us (gee, thanks) about the forthcoming explosion, telling us that it might be very big. We just laughed at them and said, "Let 'er blow!" We knew our foxholes were great protection. So the engineers strung their wire back another hundred yards and repeated, "Fire in the hole!" We all yelled, "Let 'er blow!" With a huge bang, that pillbox lifted up about an inch or two off the ground. A ton of smoke came pouring out, and we got covered in dust. What a mess—and that damn thing still wasn't destroyed. I'm not sure if they ever got that thing fully destroyed, because we moved out the next day.

We were back with our tanks crossing at Worms. Talk about heroes . . . these thousands of men risked their lives every hour of every day in combat, always under fire, for months at a time. As we lived it, we had no hope of the war ending in this foreign land. We were fighting for freedom and, in my opinion, nothing will ever surpass the misery and sacrifices endured by those who served our great country during WWII. Most of them are gone now, but we have them to thank. Our country is like no other in the history of mankind. Maybe those who try to tear it down should be treated just like the Nazis.

The Siegfried: Epilogue

In 2013 and 2014, I went back to Omaha Beach for the celebrations of the 69th and 70th anniversaries of D-Day. Visiting France, Belgium, and Luxemburg was incredible. People were overjoyed to see us and extended sincere appreciation for our service. Thousands and thousands of photos were taken, and handshakes and speeches were given. They did a fine job of decorating, and the masses pleaded for autographs.

At Bastogne—sight of so many key fights during the Battle of the Bulge—I was overwhelmed, barely able to move, by the crowd's support. I wish crowds here in the United States were half as kind and showed greater appreciation for our servicemen and women. We should all be gratified by our country's greatness.

During the 2014 tour along the Rhine River with my neighbor and friend, Joe Machol, we hit the nightclub area, where we met up with a lot of enthusiastic Frenchmen. The champagne was flowing, and a man came up to me and said he wanted to take me out to fly over the old battlefields. He apparently had rebuilt an old army artillery spotter plane, an L4 Piper.

How could I say no? We met the next morning at 10 AM. He was Dr. Guillaume Hubsch, of Reims, and his two young sons, Henry (five years old) and Richard (nine), took Joe and me in their car to the airstrip. We didn't hear a peep from those two kids. We pulled up to the hanger at the old, worn, small field. The boys helped their dad open the hanger doors and roll the plane out. She was ready to go.

Our host and pilot was actually a heart surgeon by day and of great note in the Reims region. I climbed into the front seat of that L4. We rolled along that grass field and took off, flying toward the old Siegfried Line, up by the German border.

Many wars have been fought over this land: The Gauls, Romans, Napoleon . . . World War I and World War II. Looking down at the beautiful, lush green meadows with clusters of villages in the rolling hills, I could see why. The Seine and Rhine river valleys, surrounded by pine forests, are the breadbaskets of Europe. I opened the fold-down door and took a lot of pictures.

What a glorious, sunny day we had, with just a slight breeze. What a difference sixty-nine years makes. I could almost hear all those guns still firing. Or see all those emplacements and pillboxes. They were clear in my mind's eye. . . . We left after a late lunch and headed toward our next tour destination.

> MANY WARS HAVE BEEN FOUGHT OVER THIS LAND: THE GAULS, ROMANS, NAPOLEON . . . WORLD WAR I AND WORLD WAR II. LOOKING DOWN AT THE BEAUTIFUL, LUSH GREEN MEADOWS WITH CLUSTERS OF VILLAGES IN THE ROLLING HILLS, I COULD SEE WHY.

The Bronze Star

This is how my Bronze Star Medal commendation reads:

Award of the Bronze Star Medal

By direction of the President, under the provisions of Army Regulations 600-45, 22 September 1943, as amended, the Bronze Star Medal is awarded to:

BIRNEY T. HAVEY JR.

. . . for heroic achievements in action on 20 March 1945, near Ludwigswinkel, Germany.

When our forces were pinned down by intense machine gun and rifle fire while advancing through the Siegfried Line, Private Havey volunteered to advance on

a reconnaissance for routes to by-pass the positions of re-sistance. As fire from one machine gun became so heavy that he could advance no further, he crawled to the left flank of the emplacement and threw a hand grenade into the midst of the crew, killing two and forcing a third to flee. Private Havey's heroism and courage opened a path for our advancing forces to flank the other enemy posi-tions unmolested. [Havey] entered military service from St. Louis, Missouri.

HARRY J. COLLINS
Major General, USA commanding

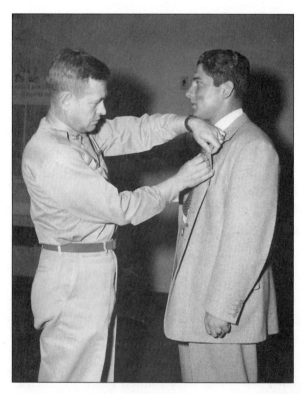

I was called to Jefferson Barracks, St. Louis, in 1948, to receive my Bronze Star. It was given for action in the Siegfried Line attack in March 1945.

HEADQUARTERS 42ND RAINBOW INFANTRY DIVISION
OFFICE OF THE COMMANDING GENERAL

30 January 1946

CITATION

AWARD OF THE BRONZE STAR MEDAL

By direction of the President, under the provisions of
Army Regulations 600-45, 22 September 1943, as amended, the
Bronze Star Medal is awarded to:

SIRKEY T. HAVEY JR.

17 075 653, Private First Class, Infantry, Anti-Tank Company,
232d Infantry for heroic achievement in action on 20 March 1945,
near Ludwigswinkel, Germany.

When our forces were pinned down by intense machine gun and
rifle fire while advancing through the Siegfried Line, Private
Havey volunteered to advance on a reconnaissance for routes to
by-pass the positions of resistance. As fire from one machine
gun became so heavy that he could advance no farther, he crawled
to the left flank of the emplacement and threw a hand grenade
into the midst of the crew, killing two and forcing a third to
flee. Private Havey's heroism and courage opened a path for our
advancing forces to flank the other enemy positions unmolested.
Entered military service from St. Louis, Missouri.

WAR DEPARTMENT   WASHINGTON, D.C.

HARRY J. COLLINS
Major General, USA

It is an honor for me to forward

this decoration

ROBERT P. PATTERSON
SECRETARY OF WAR

44

KRAVITS AND LEBECTIN

Before crossing the Rhine on General Patton's pontoon bridge, we were in a long line of troops and vehicles. We happened to be in a Jeep with the company's mail orderly and runner, both of who were Jews from up East. Their names were Kravits and Lebectin, and they had thick northeastern accents.

Movement in the line was slow. We hadn't eaten for a day or so. We weren't starving, but we were plenty hungry, I'll tell you that. We were passing through a warehouse area that hadn't been bombed too badly. I noticed an open door to one of the warehouses; GIs were coming and going freely from this building. I told Kravits and Lebectin to stay with the Jeep, because I had spotted one GI with a wine bottle, and thought I would investigate further.

Lo and behold, we had come upon a wine storage business with shelves and shelves of bottled wine, each lying flat in its holder. All the bottles were of the green champagne kind, and they weren't labeled. I decided I could easily carry three bottles inside my field jacket. Lebectin and Kravits waited while I gathered my loot.

What we really could have used was food in our bellies, but hey, beggars can't be choosers. Wine would have to do! We each drank a bottle of very white, dry Rhine wine—and we got blind drunk.

CROSSING THE RHINE

General Patton's Third Army made the assault crossing of the famous Rhine River in Oppenheim, Germany. It was a bit of a sneak assault, to get just ahead of British General Montgomery and his planned, massive crossing, dubbed Operation Plunder. Patton crossed south of Mainz, farther south on the river than Montgomery was. Our 222nd had been in reserve for a few days after our battles around Haguenau. We were riding Jeeps and half-ton trucks passing through the Third Army's Rhine bridgehead. Patton's engineers built a large pontoon boat bridge fit for troops and small vehicles.

(Worms, a German city on the Rhine River, was in the famous white wine and champagne areas, where the grapes grew on patties and fields. Man-made bluffs overlooked the river. I had the occasion on my trip back to visit some of these terraced fields, and I noticed a pile of flat white rocks at the end of each row. The farmer explained that during the grape-ripening season, they placed the white rocks on the ground below the vines containing bunches of grapes to reflect the sun up under them, to help ripen the underside of the grapes; all the rocks were laid by hand.)

So, later, our Division moved across the Rhine. Don't ask me how we drove across that narrow, weaving pontoon bridge blind drunk—but we did. We certainly had quite the hangovers kicking in, with debilitating headaches. Lebectin and Kravits kept bitching about their headaches, for hours on end. I must admit, I never had such a headache, before or since. It was one hell of a hangover.

I told Lebectin and Kravits that if they said one more word about their heads I would shoot them both in the head, and that would be that. Since I had quite the kills record and reputation, they shut up like mummies. The moral of this story is to never drink white wine on a two-day-empty stomach! If you should ever be tempted, just shoot yourself in the head first and save some time.

We were across the Rhine and on our way. This crossing was both strategic and symbolic. Everyone knew that once we crossed the Rhine, it was over for the Germans. The drive to Berlin and takedown of the rest of the German army would be inevitable—as indeed it turned out to be.

WURTZBURG

The 42nd Division advanced into Germany with our infantrymen riding atop Sherman tanks. The tanks carried 57-mm and 75-mm guns and 30-cal machine guns inside, firing frontwards. A 50-cal gun was mounted outside along the side. Our maintenance shop welded the railings to hold sandbags, giving greater protection against enemy projectiles and the German Panzer. About six men would ride on the tank, outside, with their packs tied on. Advances were much faster, and we did not have to walk, as infantry is noted for. It was more dangerous, though, as tanks were sitting ducks without infantry protection. The bazooka, Panzer Faust, and Molotov cocktails were the biggest dangers to tanks in the open, especially in cities and towns with narrow streets.

At Wurtzburg, our company was equipped with 57-mm guns and trucks. After a long advance that began at dawn, we pulled up to the grand Castle Bluffs, overlooking the Main river. Our second assault was crossing that river, and the crossing had been planned for two days. As a result, we unlimbered our cannons in the Castle yard and had a ten-mile field of fire across the city and beyond.

Wurtzburg was known to be a peaceful city with a large amount of beautiful churches, famous throughout the world. It also contained a military post with plenty of barracks and troops. We were firing across the river at targets of opportunity—which meant anything that moved. The Germans had blown up the river bridges as we approached the day before. We had some good shooting for a change, with our 57-mm guns, and received some return fire, but it wasn't accurate. Some mortar dropped in behind us. They were running out of shells.

> WE WERE FIRING ACROSS THE RIVER AT TARGETS OF OPPORTUNITY—WHICH MEANT ANYTHING THAT MOVED. THE GERMANS HAD BLOWN UP THE RIVER BRIDGES AS WE APPROACHED THE DAY BEFORE.

Monaghan and I noticed some nice homes just a few blocks to our rear. They looked prime for looting. So off we went. We needed to set up our rear defense anyhow. Lieutenant Davis came along—he was the king of looting—with a Jeep packed full of stuff. The row of homes turned out to be high military officer quarters, along with Nazi officials. The house I started to search was the commander's home. He had an extensive stamp collection—like an entire room full of books of stamps! Most of the collection ended up on the floor, though. On the wall, I found a silver plaque of Adolf Hitler, with his signature. It was about the size of a sheet of copy paper and was in a celluloid frame. I also saw a new pair of Nazi dress boots (the long ones) that fit me. The commander had a lot of medals and ribbons on display with the plaque of Hitler.

In my home today, I have this very plaque hanging on my wall.

Research revealed that this particular Hitler plaque was indeed signed by Hitler himself and had been given to the commander, one of his favorite pals. Only a very limited amount of these were made by the jeweler Hummel, the miniature China doll maker of fame. I had the plaque reframed in walnut and placed in a glass casing shadow box. (I also have my original helmet that I wore throughout the entire war—every battle and campaign—on that wall. I brought it home with me after being honorably discharged in 1947. I'll have more on my helmet near the end of this book.)

Across the River

After looting in Wurtzburg, we dug in for the night. We received orders to fall back about eighteen miles, this just before midnight. In about a half-hour, we were out of Wurtzburg and pulling back, where we dug in along the road. The British were going to bomb Wurtzburg that night, with 2,000-pound "block busters," as the Germans were still shooting and would not surrender. After midnight, the big bombers came. The first pathfinders dropped their flares, and

After midnight, the big bombers came. The first pathfinders dropped their flares, and the Royal Air Force bombed all night, one after another. We had quite the view of the four-engine bombers flying right over us and dropping bombs relentlessly.

the Royal Air Force bombed all night, one after another. We had quite the view of the four-engine bombers flying right over us and dropping bombs relentlessly. These were brave men doing their duty.

We moved back that next morning starting at dawn. Coming upon the home area we had previously looted, we saw where several of those huge bombs had hit the area, about two to three blocks from the famous castle in the region, which didn't appear to be damaged at all! (See next chapter for more about this castle.) What was left in the wake of the bombings were huge holes about half a block around and 10 to 20 feet deep. Talk about ruining a neighborhood! We re-established our original firing position and our foxholes.

Across the river were severely damaged buildings. The Germans were moving back to fight our river crossing that next morning. We did some shooting that day and readied for the boat assault the next morning. We were assembled in a railway tunnel downriver from the castle. We received quite a bit of fire from the Germans' flack wagon, which was firing 20-mm shells. (Flack wagons are German anti-aircraft guns mounted on flat-bed trailers, with four guns on each wagon. They can fire off about a thousand rounds per minute while firing in unison.) We were trapped for a while in this rail tunnel, moving upriver closer to the blown bridge.

Picking up our KIA (killed in action) and wounded, we loaded up our rubber assault boats for the cruise across the river, which covered about 60 yards. We shoved off from the broken bridge and used it for the protection of our four T6 rubber boats. The first wave of boats was one squad of men, and the Germans went in behind them and killed them all like dogs. A half-track towed a 30-mm, four-barrel flak gun trailer, and we returned fire. But by the time we got to the men, they were barbecued, the smoke still rising.

The rest of Germans left in a hurry. Good thing too, because we were mighty mad.

In Wurtzburg, House to House

We started our systematic search, block by block and house by house, for enemy . . . but also for loot. One squad was assigned per block. We never saw a single civilian. Many strange and lucky things happened to us during the war. We often wondered when our luck would run out. Every day we encountered near misses. We knew that being in the wrong place at the wrong time would be the end.

Two of us were walking down a block across the river Main, straight across from the castle. We worked up the block with our squad with about twelve men behind us, ready to shoot anything that moved. I noted a curved driveway leading into a large, open garage. As I looked in, I saw a German soldier on his knee—the guy was dead as a doornail. Stiffness had set in. He was wearing his field cap and full field pack with bayonet and canteen strapped on. I rummaged through his pack, and he had a half loaf of black bread and a can of Norwegian sardines. I hadn't eaten since the night before crossing the river, so this was a great find! I opened the sardines, broke bread, and enjoyed a great feast. While I was eating, I realized a lot of meat scraps were on the floor and ceiling. I saw a backbone with ribs and a boot with a foot in it. At this point, we started playing detective, curious to

> I RUMMAGED THROUGH HIS PACK, AND HE HAD A HALF LOAF OF BLACK BREAD AND A CAN OF NORWEGIAN SARDINES. I HADN'T EATEN SINCE THE NIGHT BEFORE CROSSING THE RIVER, SO THIS WAS A GREAT FIND!

figure out what had happened to our dinner hosts in that garage. I knocked the dead guy over, but he didn't have a mark on him. Apparently the remains of the body scattered around the garage must have been the result of suicide by tank mine. If he would have blown himself up with a grenade, he wouldn't have been scattered all over.

We never did solve the mystery of the dead guy kneeling, though. Although I've had better meals, we took what we could get. Our next objective was getting on past Wurtzburg.

* * * *

Some sixty-five years later, a few years ago, here in my home in Seabrook, I was watching the History Channel on television. The subject was the British Royal Air Force and included the bombing of Wurtzburg. The story the History Channel told angered me to the point of jumping out of my chair and screaming at the TV! You've read my eyewitness account here; whoever produced that program must be a Communist with an agenda to change the history books. They certainly didn't get the facts right. They stated that Wurtzburg didn't need to be bombed as it offered no resistance and didn't contain any troops. They also said the British firebombed the poor people of Wurtzburg. These are gross misrepresentations, unfounded and untrue statements. Period. Unfortunately, most will accept them as truths. I am here to tell you these are lies. Plenty of Nazi troops were in Wurtzburg. In fact, they had a military post with resistance firing.

The British did not firebomb it, and the city did not burn. I was watching from the ground, as were the rest of my 42nd Division mates. Don't believe everything you see on TV!

WURTZBURG CASTLE HISTORY:
THE MARIENBERG FORTRESS

So what about that castle in Wurtzburg, also known as the Marienberg Fortress? It is a large, towering stone wall structure, rising above the Main river 500 feet. In 1945, it had isolated access roadways and big steel gates. The inside courtyard was without plants or vegetation. The castle had guard portholes, from which men could stick spears or arrows for protection. The whole thing was constructed of huge stones—stones only—dark brown in color, fitted to gather perfectly.

The big foundation wall is now stair-stepped down, and grapevines grow in rows.

Wurtzburg is one of the oldest cities in southern Germany, a center of art and medical schools. It was defended by the fanatical Nazi chief of police, called the Volkstrum ("People's Army") Commander, a retired army colonel who organized the city's defense with pickup units and retreating men. Our Ranger troops required anti-tank bazooka units in the assault across the river. Guess who got that job? That was our unit.

* * * *

Upon my passing through the area coming home after the war, I noted a big 42nd Division rainbow was painted on the face above the area where we made the assault crossing during the battle. On my visit there in 2014, I looked over the Main River and noted numerous bullet holes in the bridge walls. I could see our assembly area before our crossing, the area we used sixty-nine years before! I called this to the attention of our World War II tour companions.

Quite a few men had died there in that battle; my thoughts

went out to them. I went home, and they went into mattress covers, where they remain, in some of the beautiful cemeteries of the area.

Rest Period

Following the advance into Wurtzburg, we moved out of our foxholes and bunkers and marched back to division reserve, about thirty miles from our positions on the MLR. After almost four months, it was our turn to take a break. By now, though there were still very cold nights, the days were warming.

After walking just a few miles, our trucks picked us up. We rode in style and arrived at the base, where movies, hot showers, and new uniforms awaited us.

We had gone about four months without clean clothes and very few opportunities to bathe—if you can call it that. No haircuts or shaves, either. We had used our helmets as tubs, which led to the coining of the phrase "whore's bath." I can't tell you how good that hot, clean water felt. I have no words to express how wonderful getting good and clean felt.

When I first joined the army several years earlier, I shaved twice a month, whether I needed it or not. I'm fair-skinned, with light-brown hair and blue eyes. Still, a man needs a good shave now and then, and we had gone without one for a long time.

Picking out a rest area boiled down to Captain Waters selecting a group of destroyed towns where the mess hall could be established. The showers at this particular site were set up on an acre lot with tents and mass groupings of showerheads running continuously. About twenty-four men at a time would enjoy a nice, warm shower for about ten minutes. Soap was compliments of the good ol' army, along with lots of towels to dry off. Ten minutes may not sound like much, but when you've been bathing out of a helmet, this felt like Heaven. In war, little things matter.

WE HAD USED OUR HELMETS AS TUBS, WHICH LED TO THE COINING OF THE PHRASE "WHORE'S BATH." I CAN'T TELL YOU HOW GOOD THAT HOT, CLEAN WATER FELT. I HAVE NO WORDS TO EXPRESS HOW WONDERFUL GETTING GOOD AND CLEAN FELT.

Next up was getting new uniforms, because we had about destroyed the ones we were in; they were covered in unidentifiable slime and blood, some from the enemy and some from peers. We formed a line to receive brand new coats, two pairs of *dry* socks, two pairs of undershirts, a pair of long johns, brown wool shirts, pants, a belt, overpants, jackets, wool caps, and gloves. Wholly crap, we were styling! The dirty clothes pile was about ten feet high by fifty yards long. Good riddance to that stinky pile, but I'll tell you this: if clothes could talk, the stories those rags would tell.

Monaghan and I set up company headquarters in the former mayor's house in this chosen town, because this structure had a really good roof. The windows were all bashed in except for a small back room with an eighteen-inch-wide inside door. It had a wood stove, and we found two old mattresses. Man, we were in hog heaven!

We hunted around to find some tape to seal this back window. Old farmhouses like this were built in medieval times, when straw and mud were used under the walls. Stovepipes extended through to the outside. Eventually, they started adding a plaster coating inside and out. Each improvement through time thickened the walls, making them, by the time of this war, quite bullet- and shell-proof. Combined with the tile roofs, these structures were more like forts than houses—unless, of course, they took a direct hit. In some cases, the walls were two feet thick, with deep window casements. Our new quarters were such a drastic change from being outside in the cold foxholes. We had a stove for heat and cooking, and we even had mattresses to sleep on on the dry, warm floor.

POTATO MASHERS AND PRACTICAL JOKES

They say that idle minds make for trouble; well, we were no different. Our room had an extremely small doorway leading to an inner hallway. We always wore our steel helmets inside; otherwise, we'd knock the hell out of our heads from the low doorways. We found a few German grenades, or potato mashers as we called them, because they were made of steel with a round head and wooden handle, resembling the old style of potato masher. The German grenade had a long hollow handle made of wood that screwed into the metal explosive head on one end, and a metal screw on the bottom cap. If you unscrewed the metal bottom cap, a China ring would fall out; it was attached to a rayon string. If you pulled that string, it would set off a five-second burn to an explosion. However, if you removed the tube-like cap altogether, the grenade was rendered harmless.

Monaghan and I conjured up a dummy routine where I would fool around with the disarmed grenade while he instructed me on what not to do. We would find some poor sap and make him our test subject. We'd get the fellow into a room, then run for the door. We'd end up getting stuck in the small doorway, trapping the poor guy in our room with a grenade ready to blow. Our first visitor was our company clerk back from regimental HQ, a relatively safe area. Me—the dummy—starts messing around with the potato masher grenade while Monaghan warns me not to fool around with it. I say, "What's this?" as I screw off the bottom and the string falls out, waiting to be pulled. Monaghan yells as I pull the string, drop the grenade, and we both bolt for the door. We both get to the door at the same time and get stuck. The poor clerk hits us like a freight train trying to get out. He then runs back and wraps up in one of the mattresses on the floor. Monaghan and I are falling down laughing. Our big trick went off just as planned.

> MONAGHAN YELLS AS I PULL THE STRING, DROP THE GRENADE, AND WE BOTH BOLT FOR THE DOOR. WE BOTH GET TO THE DOOR AT THE SAME TIME AND GET STUCK. THE POOR CLERK HITS US LIKE A FREIGHT TRAIN TRYING TO GET OUT.

We're now waiting for our next victim. Lo and behold, one of our company runners comes looking for something to eat. This guy, Vic, was a perfect sucker. A bottomless pit, that one; he'd go through shellfire for something to eat. Monaghan and I go through our fooling around with the grenade stick, with him yelling at me, me dropping the grenade, and us getting stuck in the doorway. Vic hits us in the back trying to get out, but when he can't go anywhere, he hops backward and jumps out the window—*through* the fucking window! Wholly crap. So much for our patch job; glass was everywhere and the stovepipe torn to bits. But we laughed our asses off. We ended up having to scrounge around for more window glass and stuff to repair the pipe.

My hand and arm were still sore and tender, as I had just returned from the division field hospital the day before. Ten days earlier, I'd been shot through the hand. But that didn't stop us from more troublemaking adventures for our idle minds and hands. Outside, we ran into Lieutenant Davis. He was from an old army family, a first-class looter, and a bit dingy. His deep trailer ended up half full of looted German hunting guns, canes, and lots more. He had a large German artillery shell that had never been used. It was a good four feet long, shaped just like a 30-cal bullet, with a brass casing about 10 inches in diameter. He wanted someone to cut off the brass casing to remove the explosive shell. His thought was that the brass casing would make an excellent upright umbrella stand for his folks' hallway in Washington, D.C. We all thought that was a good idea, and someone volunteered to hammer and chisel that son of a bitch off. We cleared the area to a safe distance until the sparks stopped flying.

Once the casing was cut off, we returned and took charge of the large amount of black powder rods, which were about three feet long. These stiff rods made quite a pile, and we started lighting them. I discovered that if you held the rod horizontal, it burned slower and longer than when vertical. We wanted to burn the entire pile, but who would light it? I got the bright idea of making one long continuous wick. Across the one-lane road was open country, so we carried the pile of powder rods to the other side of the road. We set them down, a line of joining rods crossing the road. No traffic was coming, so I was ready to light the pile when I hear a truck engine. I look down the road to see a convoy of two-and-a-half-ton trucks—six of them!—carrying replacements for our lost comrades who had been killed or wounded. I judged that the big powder burn would be over before the open trucks, with their men, passed. We had a good breeze going that was blowing across the road and into our faces. The wick kept burning, and the trucks came closer. I figured I could always just kick the wick apart and stop the fire. No problem. I looked to measure the timing again, and everything seemed fine.

> I JUDGED THAT THE BIG POWDER BURN WOULD BE OVER BEFORE THE OPEN TRUCKS, WITH THEIR MEN, PASSED. WE HAD A GOOD BREEZE GOING THAT WAS BLOWING ACROSS THE ROAD AND INTO OUR FACES. THE WICK KEPT BURNING, AND THE TRUCKS CAME CLOSER.

To this day, I do not know what happened. Did the wick slow down, or did the trucks accelerate? About the time the first and second open trucks came by, a big flame shot up about fifteen feet high, and it bent across the road and across those trucks. *Shit!* I still can see the truck driver's eyes bulging out in shear fear. Ha! They just kept going, and Monaghan and I just stood there watching like dummies. We finally walked away to hide, and we never heard a word about it.

I still wonder what those new replacements must have thought. But this adventure is one we kept quiet about.

On the Road By Nuremberg/Furth

April 18, 1945

The 222nd Anti-Tank Unit of the Rainbow Division had developed into a tank-riding attack force. Flankers would go on side roads to keep contact with attacking groups to our left and right flanks, preventing us from barging into a trap. We followed a two-lane, asphalt road to a long valley in the sloping hills. The mortar fire (the mortar is a small tube that lobs shells high in the air at the enemy; it's operated by a three-man team) and sniper roadblocks became less and less. Our confidence was increasing. Hell, we might actually get out of this alive! Soon that would be reality.

OUR CONFIDENCE WAS INCREASING. HELL, WE MIGHT ACTUALLY GET OUT OF THIS ALIVE! SOON THAT WOULD BE REALITY.

I was in the middle of a group

stretching about a mile long. The order came down to stop or hold up. Our captain gave orders to feed this company of about 250 men. The HQ and mess supply trucks pulled off the road and we spread out along the road some 400 yards away. For some reason, we did not dig foxholes. When we stopped to take a piss, we never knew if we would be called in ten minutes or ten hours. The drill went like this: Post out flankers, set up defensive positions, and dig in. Pick your field of fire and set up for an attack from your enemy. The nights were still frosty, and mist settled in at dusk. We scrounged up some wood and built fires along the line.

As dusk settled in, the comfort of warm food felt great, but our combat experience told us we were taking a stupid chance sitting along a road and cooking with open fires, all without cover. Sure enough, I heard the whine of a diving aircraft. Our fires created a perfect line of sight and target from the air. HQ First Platoon, the third platoon in line, took fire. They hadn't dug in either. The German Messerschmitt 109 coming at us poured small 30-mm and 30-caliber on the entire bonfire line. Everyone dove under a truck, and we heard a loud blast. I thought it was a bomb. The tracers passed just one of our positions. Our first sergeant, Witrode, yelled, "Put out the damn fires!" I was already up and kicking out the fires and yelled back at him to get his ass out from under the truck and help.

I heard the 109 turning around for another pass, but actually, it turned out to be the 109's wing mate coming around to join him! All fires were out now, and I unlimbered the 50-cal machine gun on the supply truck's right front fender. I opened up the ammo box, stuffed my belt on the left side, cocked twice, and popped off two or three rounds. I pointed up toward the aircraft's sound and its run path. I waited for the plane's muzzle to flash. Instead, he flew off. However, I caught a whiff of the strong gasoline smell all around us. Monaghan, our company clerk, came staggering out of the radio truck, a three-quar-ter-ton-covered model with a long antenna. He said, "He hit me." Another GI came in and said that the plane had crashed about 40 yards away. I followed him over that way, noticing a big gouge out of the ground where the 109 fighter had first hit the terrain firing. We came up to a ten-yards-long, four-foot-wide, and three-foot-deep cavity with gasoline all about, still evaporating, along with oil. Monaghan was acting better and more like himself as we looked over the wreckage. The German 109 aircraft had indeed crashed. As we surveyed the tail with its Nazi markings about 40 yards away, we saw the fuselage, its top half, and the pilot still in it. The pilot's legs and hips were gone. I guess his guts went with his legs. This all happened at night, mind you, but we had developed a pretty keen ability to see in the dark, which served us well in combat situations. In fact, a light at night was somewhat of an irritation.

This pilot's upper torso was intact. He was wearing a brand new leather flight jacket, which I took off of him in a matter of min-utes. It was like new, with only a couple of drops of blood on it. The black and white fur inside looked like Persian lamb, and the light, white skin was so soft on the outside. I gathered the waist and zipper front with a large flap type of collar. I later packed it into my barracks bag with the supply truck so I could get that jacket home to St. Louis. Home was something most fellas didn't give too much thought to during combat. We didn't have the time, for one, but we also didn't want to be reminded of all we had left behind. Yes, we were fighting for ones we loved, and we were damn proud to

> THIS PILOT'S UPPER TORSO WAS INTACT. HE WAS WEARING A BRAND NEW LEATHER FLIGHT JACKET, WHICH I TOOK OFF OF HIM IN A MATTER OF MINUTES.

do so. But thinking too much about those loved ones was dangerous. It made you vulnerable, and that could get you killed.

(Later, back in St. Louis, I wore that pilot's jacket while hunting in the area. Quail hunting was my main delight, but that took a lot of walking with your dogs, so the pilot's jacket was actually too warm. It had a big pull-up collar that just was not practical for any of my activities, so it just hung in a closet at home for years. I think my mother phased it out. I wish I had it now among my other souvenirs brought home from the ETO.)

Back at the scene of the crash, Monaghan took me over to the company radio truck. I could see where that German 109 struck the upper left side of the canvas and wood roof bar, tearing out two feet of canvas and shattering the wood curve of the roof's support bar with his wing or prop. It must have struck Monaghan in the helmet; there was a dent.

Although this battle was only fifteen minutes in length, some unbelievable things happened:

1. The pilot was killed in the crash, coming down right alongside us.
2. We only had three wounded soldiers.
3. We were covered with aviation gas and did not explode.
4. The pilot was cut in half; however, his jacket remained intact. Lucky me.
5. Monaghan was sitting in the radio truck, which was struck by the aircraft wing, but he was not injured at all, suffering only a dent in his helmet!

Who could believe such things could happen, all within the space of a few minutes? But this was war. Anything was possible.

A Letter to Mom

I sent this letter to Mrs. B.T. Havey Sr., 4629 Margaretta, St. Louis, in April 1945.

It has the typical stamp in which it was passed by a U.S. examiner. It's an example of typical GI correspondence from the ETO.

4/25/45

Dear Mom,

Don't mind this pen. I'm just keeping you posted as well as I can.

We had a bit of rain. It became quite cold also. Just our luck to be out in it for three days & nights.

I received another box from you. It came

to me the first night. Boy did that w[h]iskey come in good. How about another shipment[?].

We knocked down a German plane last nite. It was shooting at us and came in too low. He crashed about 15 yards from me. Knocked off my pal's helmet with his wing. It's hard to believe I know, but it did happen.

The kid said he would paint a plane on his helmet. All in a day's work.

Received a letter from Bud Walker also. Well, tell all hello.

Drop me a line soon.
Love, Bud

THE WOMEN
OF EUROPE

The war was becoming easier, and the weather was getting warmer. Somewhere along the road after Wurtzburg's capture, we halted inside a small town. It was pitch-black, and we became mixed in with a truck convoy carrying slave labor from the camps. We hardly ever saw civilians, but I met this cute little gal. She started flirting with me, holding onto my left arm, which was still tender from the wound I had got more than a month back. We were right near a big truck, so we hopped into the front cab and started kissing. I couldn't believe I was really feeling a woman's body. We both got pretty heated up, and things went the full way from there. . . . After all that I had been through, I thought surely I had died and gone to Heaven.

You could say we stayed up in that cab quite a long time, long enough to go at it again. And then, it was time to go. Before she left, I gave her one big kiss. Down the street she went, into the

German darkness. All these years, I have wondered whatever happened to her. Did she get home OK? Did she even have a home? She said she was from Czechoslovakia and had been a slave laborer for four years. She told me she was twenty-one and had just been set free the day before when our 42nd Division overran the camp.

Adolf Hitler affected the lives of millions upon millions. To him, life meant nothing. Other Germans acted like they didn't know what was going on, but I'm not buying it. Ants know what is happening in their anthill. After all we'd been through, after all the evil perpetrated by that man, we didn't mind finally getting to enjoy ourselves in his country.

Throughout the war, we were ordered not to fraternize with the Germans—whatsoever. As I said, we saw many while we were fighting and shooting in battle. Otherwise, we rolled along, living off the land. We got eggs, chickens, and anything else we could find to eat. Germans in the country lived a pretty good life. One day, we shot up a roadblock strong point. Just beyond it was a big farm with a large, stone barn and house. My pal, Monaghan, and I searched it for German soldiers, food, and loot. We found a small man, about fifty, working in the barn. He explained he was a Polish laborer. I could understand and speak a little German, so we talked for a few minutes. I gave him a few cigarettes. A moment later, in comes the farmer's daughter. She had been feeding the chickens. She was a blue-eyed blonde knockout, wearing a

ALL THESE YEARS, I HAVE WONDERED WHATEVER HAPPENED TO HER. DID SHE GET HOME OK? DID SHE EVEN HAVE A HOME? SHE SAID SHE WAS FROM CZECHOSLOVAKIA AND HAD BEEN A SLAVE LABORER FOR FOUR YEARS.

blue-flowered country dress with a white blouse and suspenders—like something out of a movie.

Monaghan was taking all this in and rolling his eyes. I told the girl to come with me, and we headed down toward the house Monaghan and I had just searched. She followed me a few paces behind, walking with her hands behind her back, like she probably always did. The sun was shining and made her blonde hair shimmer like gold. She had a beautiful face and was so calm and serene. We entered the house, walked across the living room, headed up the stairs, and went straight to a bedroom with a big bed that had white sheets. I told her to take off her clothes, and she did. She hung everything up neatly. Wow. What an incredible body she had . . .

Monaghan was waiting downstairs for me. I came down and gave him the thumbs up, suggesting he go up for seconds. I didn't have to tell him twice. Up the stairs he ran, leaving me with his helmet, gun, gun belt, and jacket to watch. I heard the girl shouting, "No, no officer!" Apparently, she wouldn't go to bed with any officers. Poor Monaghan had corporal stripes on his OD shirt, so he was out of luck that day.

A few hours later, we reassembled, and off to war we went again, riding on those tanks. I never got her name, first or last. A little Birney might have been running around those hills in the years right after the war. I'll never know.

* * * *

I have to be honest: the womanizing adventures didn't end there. We now jump ahead to the ending of the war.

We were in the mountains of Tyrol, training to go over and kill off the Japs. We were still chasing Nazi holdouts and SS, which kept us in the war theater for the better part of ten more months. I had some pretty good firefights when we caught up with them. We were trying to ensure our safety and end this war. Resupply and food is everything in the Alps.

I received a letter from my mom, and she said she was glad the war was over and that we were safe. She had no idea what we faced, chasing the holdouts, and that we were still in harm's way. If we found SS men, we shot them on the spot. Their tattoos were an "SS" in their left armpit. We asked men to open their shirts, and if we saw the SS, they were done. So long and goodbye. Sometimes, we would bash their skulls with the butts of our guns before killing them. You have to understand the mind-set. This wasn't happening every day, but this was post-Dachau (my account of Dachau is coming in the next chapter), so we did not feel sorry for any Germans. We liberated part of the infamous Dachau Concentration Camps and saw evil, pure evil. They didn't get our sympathy. We were half crazy by then anyhow; we just didn't know it.

> WE DID NOT FEEL SORRY FOR ANY GERMANS. WE LIBERATED PART OF THE INFAMOUS DACHAU CONCENTRATION CAMPS AND SAW EVIL, PURE EVIL. THEY DIDN'T GET OUR SYMPATHY.

Getting back to my romantic adventures, RAS—whom I will not identify further because I don't know his exact background—was a war pal. For a time, we lived in an Austrian schoolhouse with four to six rooms. The rows of desks were removed, and bunk beds were installed to make barracks for us. We had a good mess hall that served food, and inside toilets, showers, and wash bowls. Life was good!

RAS and I went for a walk around the town. We were not armed, as the war had been over for two months or so. Down a lane we met two good-looking German girls, also out for a stroll. We got to know them, and they invited us to their trailer parked under a big tree in the woods on the edge of town. We sat outside as darkness fell. Each of us had chosen a girl and the heating up began. RAS was already at it with his girl. The bunks were about thirty inches apart in the rear of the trailer, so I went to work with my gal. She loved it, we both did. . . . It was pitch- black outside the trailer. After a while, I started to smell something foul, like spoiled fish. Turns out, RAS had his fingers, arm, and hand under my nose. I let him know exactly what I thought about that! We laughed pretty hard, then went to the sink to clean up.

RAS wanted to have his way with my girl, so we planned a switch in the dark. RAS had long hair, and I had a crew cut. When my new gal rubbed my head, the gig was up. Everything came to a halt. One of the gals lit an oil lamp, saw what we were trying to do, and kicked us out. RAS and I could hardly walk home from laughing so hard. That's a little story never shared before, until now, some seventy years later.

* * * *

Our schoolhouse barracks were across from a plum orchard. Lines of blue plum trees and well-cut grass went as far as the eye could see. We had been waiting for the plums to ripen. One night, I told RAS they looked ready, and we developed our plans for a raid. You'd have thought we were establishing a combat mission patrol! It wasn't, but we were supposed to be in the barracks for the night by 7 PM for bed checks. Instead, our secret mission began at dark. We crossed the road, went over a fence, and walked under those big trees, where we started eating fallen plums. They were so sweet! We ate our fill of those blue plums, which were about the size of a ping-pong ball.

We had our helmets on, so we figured we'd bring some

plums back for the guys. RAS and I filled our helmets about three quarters of the way full. We climbed back over the fence and into our bunk area in the schoolhouse. A lot of guys came around to get some plums. We poured hundreds of blue plums on top of a bunk blanket—and wouldn't you know it, each and every one of them had wiggly white worms in them! RAS and I had eaten about twenty-five plums in the dark. I couldn't find a single plum without a worm in it. Not one! You can imagine how we heard about being wormy . . . for days. We didn't live that raid down for a while.

So it was back to chocolate Mars bars and Babe Ruths for us. Apparently, the Germans make a plum brandy, but you won't get me to try it. I know about the worms.

Schweinfurt Air Raid and My Salute to the 8th and 9th Air Force

During the long winter war I was able to see quite a few air raids. It seemed that any given, clear day we could see the B-17 Bombers on their way back and forth from bombing German targets. Their long contrails filled the sky; they were way up above 30,000 feet.

From the 8th and 9th Air Force, based all over England, they were flying out to bomb or strafe with fighter planes, P-51s along with B-26 twin-engine bombers, nicknamed Marauders. The B-26 was easy to identify as it had a high tail with a thin body, a tail gunner with twin 50-cal machine guns. The front, below the pilot, carried the bombardier, a complete glass-front with two more 50-cal machine guns. These were low-level bombers, more like fighter-bombers. Their front guns could strafe oncoming targets, and they could clean up with the rear guns. Low-level bombing and strafing is about as dangerous a mission as you can get. Ground fire is deadly, as everyone is shooting at you with all types of weapons, especially the quad 30-mil flak guns—the Germans had a lot of those.

The B-26 Marauders flew fast and low like bees, usually in a diamond formation of fours. If they located a target, it was hell to pay. We saw them flying often, but nothing like the raids during our assault on April 9-11, 1945, at Schweinfurt, Germany. The 8th Air Force lost 50,000 men during the war; that's equal to two infantry divisions. Each man knew what his chances were, but those brave men gave their lives. You talk about heroes.

> THE B-26 MARAUDERS FLEW FAST AND LOW LIKE BEES, USUALLY IN A DIAMOND FORMATION OF FOURS. IF THEY LOCATED A TARGET, IT WAS HELL TO PAY.

As time passes, it seems to me that with the passing of our soldiers and eyewitnesses, their sacrifice becomes dimmer, like in our other wars. Today, however, we have better photos and records. I think, and I would hope, that our schools would advocate more commemoration of these deeds in the interest of national pride, and for maintaining the history of our country. What if we had lost? It's a simple and yet profound question: *What if we had lost this war?*

* * * *

Before I describe our activities in the Schweinfurt capture, I would like to dash ahead seventy long years, to our presidential invitation to celebrate the 70th anniversary of D-Day in France, the invasion of Europe on June 6, 1944. Before leaving for Europe for that trip, I was invited by Texas Lt. Gov. David Dewhurst, and his wife Patricia, to dinner at their home here in

Houston. The dinner and event was also a chance to meet with the French delegation from the Cherbourg province—this was the area impacted by the original invasion.

My friend Joe Machol, his aide Heather, and my daughter Jamie Ford attended the dinner. The Dewhursts were amazingly generous, and I was indeed honored. We made plans to meet again in France during the June 6 celebration. It was very special to me because Dewhurst's father was a captain and flew one of those B-26 Bombers. His father lost his life in an auto accident when David was three years old, an indescribable loss. David's dad few eight missions during D-Day alone, in and around Utah Beach, France. The French locals made efforts to develop a museum at the Utah Beach invasion location. The Dewhurst family became involved in the museum, where contributions soon erected a beautiful building, just off the English Channel, the site where David's dad had attacked so bravely with his bombing, right on that spot, cleaning out the German defenders, saving our soldiers' lives by the hundreds, and allowing our U.S. troops to advance up those beaches. Talk about heroes.

The museum is located on the edge of a sand slope. Inside is a full-size B-26 Bomber, guns ready, wheels down, one of many displays of a once-in-a-lifetime invasion of a continent that occurred 70 years earlier.

* * * *

What is the connection between Birney Havey and the B-26 Bomber called the Marauder? First, this: 5,288 B-26s were built for the war. They carried 5,800 pounds of bombs, just under three tons, in their bellies. When the sun shines at Utah Beach on the French shore, the translucent roof of the museum lights up, almost cathedral-like, and shines down on that B-26 at rest in the main room of the *musee* (French for museum).

It was a sunny, spring-like day, warm and the sun shining on our backs, on April 9, 1945. Our company jumped off; we were on the top, riding the lead assault tanks at about dawn. The attack on Schweinfurt from our artillery had been firing ahead for hours. We rode along the edge of a long woods to our left; our mission was to kill anything that moved to our front. As the sun came up, our front was a long, sloping flat plain and our view was for about 12 miles ahead of us.

WE RODE ALONG THE EDGE OF A LONG WOODS TO OUR LEFT; OUR MISSION WAS TO KILL ANYTHING THAT MOVED TO OUR FRONT. AS THE SUN CAME UP, OUR FRONT WAS A LONG, SLOPING FLAT PLAIN AND OUR VIEW WAS FOR ABOUT 12 MILES AHEAD OF US.

The Germans had four or five clusters of 88-mm anti-aircraft on our side, protecting Schweinfurt's great ball-bearing plants—these plants were the main targets. We could see those German guns firing skyward, high up in the sky. We could see the contrails of the B-17 Bombers on their missions, bombing sections of Schweinfurt. Here comes the B-26 low-level bomber sweeping across. We could see our—and their—fighters. The B-26s flew in diamond formations of four; Hollywood could never truly duplicate this panoramic scene that was unfolding in front of us.

The German 88s were all firing; the tanks on which we were riding were within range, their 75-mm cannons firing. The aircraft machine guns were firing; the German mortars were firing back at us. All this hell of war, but soon, the German defense was overwhelmed by our forces. Parts of shot-up aircraft were falling out of the sky, tinsel radar-blocking foil was falling, and the B-26 Bombers were making their drops at the edge of Schweinfurt. They broke up for a strafing, 50-cal run.

Dust smoke started to cover our objective. Our tanks took us to the edge of town, where we unloaded for house-to-house cleanup. Through all of this, we had yet to lose a man, but that magic didn't last long; we had many blocks and factories to go through to end that aircraft death trap forever.

The 9th of April 1945. A scene I'll never forget. In my research of B-26 missions for this book, I found that Captain Dewhurst's wing was indeed flying that mission. That would have put Lieutenant Governor Dewhurst's father within a few short miles of our 42nd Division, 222nd Infantry, fighting on the ground, Birney Havey among those troops that day. Unbelievable?

Now I am 93 years old and these events are still fresh in my mind. My book title—*Never Left the Battlefields*—is again affirmed in these memories, in this chapter, in the Battle for Schweinfurt. So many of our fliers in the 8th and 9th Air Force

SO MANY OF OUR FLIERS IN THE 8TH AND 9TH AIR FORCE GAVE THEIR LIVES AND THEIR TOMORROWS, ALONG WITH MY BRAVE COMRADES, DOWN IN THE DIRT, DUST, AND SQUALOR OF BATTLE.

gave their lives and their tomorrows, along with my brave comrades, down in the dirt, dust, and squalor of battle.

SCHWEINFURT: EPILOGUE

There were a lot of heroes in that battle. My mind goes back to the dinner at Lieutenant Governor Dewhurst's, before our trip back in the spring for the 70th anniversary of D-Day. Earlier that day, I was honored at the Houston Texans vs. San Diego Chargers football game. Both former President George W. Bush and Dewhurst gave me a standing ovation. Apparently, I was a high-profile hero! Besides me, two prisoners of war were also in attendance, and we greeted the French delegation from the museum at Omaha Beach in France. The Dewhurst family was a significant contributor and sponsor of the war museum, as I wrote, which contains that full-scale, intact B-26 Bomber with wheels down and guns aimed, ready to fly. That plane is just like one that Dewhurst's father would have flown.

I enjoyed meeting the French delegation at that invitation-only affair and dinner at the Dewhursts' home in Houston. Also among the delegation was the curator of the Utah Beach Museum, Ingrid Anquetil. She served as the French translator for the party since most of the delegates only spoke French. French national television was there as well, and they interviewed me quite a bit. I guess I'm well known on French TV now! Also in attendance at that dinner as part of the French legation was Jean-Francois Le Grand, president of the General Council of the Manche region; Marc Lefevre, mayor of Saint-Mere-Eglise; and Henri Milet, mayor of Sainte-Marie-du-Mont. It was quite the Who's Who!

* * * *

I'd like to relate one final story that involves that famous 8th Air Force. During our spring tour of the area for the 70th anniversary celebration, one of our stops was Erwin Rommel's headquarters, which was in the heavily German-occupied part of France during that time. General Rommel was a German hero who directed massive battles in North Africa and was later appointed to defend the west coast of France against the allies.

Rommel chose an old castle that sat in a mountain valley for his headquarters. It was built into the side wall of a big bluff, more than a hundred years ago. It was located about 150 miles from the English Channel defenses of that forthcoming invasion. Built from local stone, it was a typical medieval defensive castle with a big row of gates, a moat, and tall walls with a great deal of separation from the front.

Although secure, I think air safety was in question. Rommel was shot and wounded in his car, by our planes, a gain for that famous 8th Air Force that flew out of England. That, however, is not what killed him, though I think he never came back from those wounds. As history tells us, he later got involved in a plot to assassinate Hitler, which led to his forced suicide (he was given the choice of his own suicide, with honor following), or to be tried, at which he would be found guilty, executed, all his staff executed, and his family also made to suffer. Rommel committed suicide in October 1944 (before I ever got to Europe). And with his death, a large state funeral was held for him.

Dachau and
the Jews

Before diving into this piece of my history with the 222nd, I'd like to paint a little context of how Jews were viewed around the world in the 1930s and 1940s.

My childhood neighborhood is still etched in my mind. I remember clearly the clean streets lined with brick houses built of white limestone; all the houses had basements. Many of the steps leading to the front porches were made of white stone from a local quarry. Growing up, I had the chore of scrubbing those white stairs with this certain powder, and I did it every Saturday. Those neighborhoods back then were nicknamed the "Scrubbie Dutch." I guess that was because those porches were scrubbed clean, and we had a lot of Dutch in those neighborhoods.

Those are some childhood memories. It was a time when America was growing, solidifying itself as one of the top world powers, but we were also impacted by news from around the world. We were all hearing more about Hitler being in power through our local radio stations and newspapers, as I mentioned earlier. I vividly recall the news story of a 1,000 Jews who rented an ocean liner in Holland in hopes of escaping the Nazis. The Germans allowed them to board the ship since they were less than subpar humans by their standards. I believe the ship departed from Antwerp. Their escape was not successful, and the news media blasted the story, pictures and all. They wanted to dock at and enter England, but they were refused. They tried Spain and Portugal, and got the same rejection. They decided to set sail for the United States and entered the port at Fort Lauderdale, Florida. President Roosevelt would not let them off the boat. We saw images of these people begging to enter our country because of persecution. They were forced to leave and headed to Cuba, but they were even rejected there! Ultimately, they sailed back to Holland, where the Nazis hauled them off to slave camps. Later, many of these same people would be sent to their deaths in ovens. No one wanted a bunch of Jews in their country—this was how it played out around the world. I later found out that the ship that bore them around the Atlantic and back, was, ironically, named the *SS St. Louis*.

Some of the history programs claim that the ocean liner only docked in Cuba, but those of us who were of age during the war remember the hard truth. The U.S. turned them away as well. Personally, I had no issues with these people or with their faith. I worked as a stock boy for a store owned by a Jewish family. My wages were 25 cents per hour, or twelve dollars a week, if you worked all day on Saturday. They paid me by cash in a small brown envelope. They were up-and-up-type people, and even deducted social security from my pay, which was impressive since this was a fairly new thing in the 1930s.

Here's a bit of a funny story from my days as a stock boy

working for that Jewish family. One day at the H. Frager's Building, which was three stories high, I was filling orders. I was opening boxes of ladies' lingerie, receiving them into inventory, and filing paperwork. Up and down those three flights of stairs I would go, sometimes using the big freight elevator. The elevator doors opened on each floor. They were counter-weighted to glide easily. However, if the elevator was not at your floor, the door wouldn't open. It stayed locked down. The doors were solid, light plywood and painted red with a pull strap at the bottom to raise the door with a handle. On one particular day, I was busy with a large shipment of women's lingerie and silk panties that came in boxes the size of today's cereal boxes. (I had to stamp the box face with our catalog numbers, which was done on the third floor. I then had to go to the second floor to stock the shelves.) I picked up a stack of six boxes and headed for the elevator. I raised the door with my foot and stepped in. The elevator was not there; it was down on the first floor. Down I fell— with ladies' panties flying everywhere. I landed on the wire mesh top of the freight elevator! I looked up and saw everyone peeking down from the third floor to see where I had landed from that crash. Luckily, I didn't hit a thing, nor did I have a scratch on me. We lost a few pairs of panties that day, but what the hell! Someone had left the door switch open and, of course, no one owned up to it. Birney Havey lived another day.

I didn't mind working for that Jewish family. The point was, we had no problems with those of the Jewish race and religion. We couldn't understand why Hitler hated them so. And hate them he did. He aroused the anti-Semitic hate in the German people. I am still astounded how Germans everywhere claimed they never knew about the death camps, even though thousands and thousands of Germans worked in them as troop guards and in conducting trains.

I get beyond infuriated when some people claim these camps

never even happened. I've been there, folks. I've seen them firsthand. In fact, the images still haunt me to this day.

* * * *

Our combat path brought my company directly into the town of Dachau, which was about ten miles before the prison camp. Our squad was riding on a Mark 4 Sherman Tank and had come to a crossroads. The Germans had dug in a tank trap across the roadway, a bluff on one side and a big drop-off on the other. The trap was two rows of big, thick logs sunk in up and down the road. We came around the hill corner, and they opened up fire on us with rifles. Some guys on the tank behind us were hit. We instinctively slid off the safe side of the tank, out of the line of fire. We scooted along the far ditch, working our way up to a fork in the road, noting four bicycles hidden to allow the Germans a means to escape. (Interestingly, you can find a photo of exactly this type of scene—I am not sure if it is this exact moment or not—in the book I have referred to, *42nd Rainbow Infantry Division: WWII History*, where our infantry found bicycles that Germans had hidden along a hillside as a means of quick escape.) We crossed the road and had them outflanked. We had a clear view of them, looking into their slit trench, about fifty yards away. Four of them were aiming and shooting at our tank, so four of us took aim and fired our rifles at them, just like they were sitting quail. It was over in seconds. Our first shots killed them all.

We walked over to see if they had any pistols or watches. Our stalled tank column brought up the tank with the bulldozer

I GET BEYOND INFURIATED WHEN SOME PEOPLE CLAIM THESE CAMPS NEVER EVEN HAPPENED. I'VE BEEN THERE, FOLKS. I'VE SEEN THEM FIRSTHAND. IN FACT, THE IMAGES STILL HAUNT ME TO THIS DAY.

blade to break up the roadblock. That operation took about an hour, and we assessed our damages. Two men were wounded. Just down the road to the left was the town of Dachau. We knew nothing about the death camps at this point, so you can imagine the shock and horror when it came.

Information was sporadic at best when in battle, and when were we not in some sort of fight? We did have a strange fellow travel with us. He wore a regular khaki uniform with no insignias or markings. He spoke with an accent and said he was from Hungary. I suspected he was a Jew. Later, when we stumbled upon the death camp, I thought we would have to shoot him because he went completely berserk. Upon entering the camp, he grabbed a gun and shot four Jewish guards who worked for the Germans. Turns out, he was a spy or special agent for the Jews.

> WE KNEW NOTHING ABOUT THE DEATH CAMPS AT THIS POINT, SO YOU CAN IMAGINE THE SHOCK AND HORROR WHEN IT CAME.

* * * *

Before the prison camp, it's worth relaying an unusual story from the night before we reached the concentration camp. Maybe because of what happened, it took a bit of the edge off of what we would see the next day. Not much, but maybe just a bit.

We made camp for the night at the Dachau city limits. We dug in and set up guard posts. I took over a nice house on the corner where a woman, two kids, and their grandma lived. They were kicked out of the main house and told to retreat to the basement. I went directly to the kitchen and found bacon. They had a wood stove, and I got busy cooking up some bacon and eggs. Oh, the smell of that bacon on that big iron frying pan was heavenly! Me and the guys were all drooling, just waiting for the bacon to get to the right crispness.

Just then some German shells hit nearby. They were timed-fire, meaning they would explode *before* they hit the ground. We were fairly safe in the house, unless we got a direct hit. No telling what would happen then. We stayed away from the windows and got ready for a ground counterattack. One piece of shrapnel blasted through a window and landed smack dab in our frying pan. What were the chances? *Bam!* Bacon and grease splattered, and a fire burst out on top of the wood stove. Son of a bitch! By the time we got the fire out in the kitchen, our meal was destroyed. No bacon. No eggs. Zip. We ate the best we could, but we were all craving that damn bacon.

We didn't encounter any additional counterattacks from the Germans, and we were back on the road to Dachau and the prison camp the next morning.

Dachau Concentration Camp

So we had received our orders to Dachau. We were to advance through the so-called "internment camp" at Dachau; our tanks were again in line, waiting to give us a ride. As I've said, tanks need infantry for protection, and the Germans' Panzer Fausts ("tank fists") and Molotov cocktails (Russian bottles of gasoline, burning)—both of these were used by the Germans against our tank lines, and they could be done so in a somewhat effective and deadly way. One man hiding in a ditch could rise up and throw one of those cocktails onto a big armored tank and set it on fire. Same with a Panzer Faust; one shot into the right place on the side of a tank could destroy it.

So our tankers were always glad to have us riding on the outside, and we were glad to have a ride instead of hiking, which we often did anyhow. As we went down the road toward the camp, we received some incoming mortar fire, but it was sporadic and unaimed, falling off to the side and beyond, fired by retreating Germans.

I was riding atop the second tank in the column. We crossed the railroad tracks, where it was decided by our commander to split our column, half on the road and half to follow the tracks. Following the tracks, we came into sight of barbed-wire fencing. Inside were long warehouse-type structures, one story each. We then noticed a large rail yard with hundreds of boxcars . . .

We first noticed the stink and odor of . . . excuse me, but this was war. We noticed the odor of shit and oil and whatever else. Our lead tank men were leaping off and down and firing. Still about 50 yards off, we pulled up and got into a scout advance and moved up toward the fence gate and the first warehouse with its open doors. As we advanced, some prisoners ran off and started killing a few guards in uniform. The prisoners were walking skeletons in striped pullovers.

> ALL THE WHILE, WE HAD BEDLAM AMONG THE PRISONERS AS THEY CONTINUED TO MOVE CLOSER TO US . . . CHEERING, CRYING, BEGGING. THOSE POOR CREATURES WHO COULD STILL WALK . . . THEY WERE IN ALL STAGES OF STARVATION, SOME IN BETTER SHAPE THAN OTHERS. I THINK OF THAT MISERY OFTEN.

They brought us two guards; we shot them out of hand. We were starting to comprehend what kind of place this camp was. All the while, we had bedlam among the prisoners as they continued to move closer to us . . . cheering, crying, begging. Those poor creatures who could still walk . . . they were in all stages of starvation, some in better shape than others. I think of that misery often.

Lieutenant Russell Fielding started opening rail boxcars and they were full of dead, starved Jews, their contorted bodies all lying in the straw in the locked railcars. They all looked the same. I can still see them to this day. One of my company officers took pictures. The smell was offensive, and it never leaves you. Dead bodies, rotten and burned bodies, everywhere.

The bedlam continued; every once in a while a skeletal bunch would bring in a prisoner and beat him to death. As this prisoner was well fed, it was obvious he had been cooperating with the German guards. As we moved forward, we all stuck together, moving in a box-like formation, looking out for each other. No one had to give that order. Our tankers started to drift in and look around, and we noted another division coming in from the front gate direction. The bedlam started to quiet down some. . . . But the more we looked, the more we started to realize the unbelievable.

. . . More of those railcars. As doors were slid open some of the dead, starved bodies would fall out and onto the tracks; they had to be tossed back into the cars. The stench was overwhelming. . . . Our troops started to ease up and look around more; two or three of them would form a group to look over the unbelievable sights. We were hard, battle-tested, half-frozen, half-starved, dog tired at times, tough, fighting troops, and we had faced death many times. But how in the hell could you absorb this? And truthfully, we had seen nothing yet.

The camp was laid out like a city, well planned and adapted for the extermination of human beings on a large scale. Looking down a street of these long buildings, the streets about three football fields long each, the buildings were about a hundred feet long and thirty feet wide. Upon entering and stepping over dead bodies in and outside, the bunks and sleeping areas were filled with bodies that were stacked in there like mail in mail slots. Heads of the dead or those who were too weak and dying were sticking out of the bunks, four to six people or bodies in each three-foot-by-three-foot slot. There was waste and vomit laying throughout the bunks. There were hundreds in each building . . . And there was not one building, but thirty to fifty of them—tar paper-like, flat buildings with skeletons lying outside among the dead. Among those still living, with their bones and ribs sticking out, obviously beyond starving, it was hard to figure out how some could even walk, but some did, as if on stilts.

Some weren't able to walk. In the barracks, they were crammed in like sardines. I spoke a little German and communicated to people to get out.

About that time, we started to get some fire from the north side. We moved along the railroad tracks. They dropped some mortar on us, but the German army was fleeing. Most officers and guards had already left. We attacked the German guards and killed them. We found more of the prisoners who were well fed and believed to be on the Germans' side. Many of them ended up in a moat alongside the camp.

We entered a large brick and stone building: a shower/gas chamber. It was about a hundred feet by a hundred feet. There were a hundred or so dead bodies, all stacked up, like cordwood ready for the ovens. There were steel-wheeled carts to convey the bodies next door to the ovens, where there were big iron doors and a track that would run into the flames to speed up the roasting to ashes. There were stacks of oven-ready bodies in that room also. The ovens were operated by gas. Most of the dying weighed only forty to fifty pounds by the time they took their last breath and were stacked up. It seemed the ovens had been run day and night. All four ovens looked the same, and so did the people: men and women looked alike.

For years after I have often contemplated how many bodies those three or four ovens could have burned to ashes in a 24-hour period, going full blast for weeks, months, and even years. And that problem still exists in my mind; seventy years later, I will still turn those numbers over and over in my head. I think I have a phenomenal long-term memory, for both the good and the bad—and that memory still takes me back to Dachau, 1945.

* * * *

By now, the inmates had raided the guards' kitchen and food storage, where they brought out hundreds of cans of food, much of it a type of meat hash. But they had no way to open the cans! I carried my trench/bayonet knife on my ankle, strapped in its scabbard; it was very sharp. I pulled it out and cut open those cans until I had blisters. Others relieved me in cutting open those cans; there were long lines of prisoners waiting for food, by the hundreds. (I still have that same knife, a souvenir among others, hanging on display at my home here in Seabrook.)

> WE MOVED THROUGH THE CAMP, STILL IN DISBELIEF AT WHAT WE WERE SEEING. THERE WAS JUST NO END TO THE HUNGER AND NEED.

We moved through the camp, still in disbelief at what we were seeing. There was just no end to the hunger and need. At this point, we didn't have any medical assistance, or any real direction of any type, for that matter, to help these people.

Some of the din and excitement had died down at the camp. We had no orders to move out, so we prepared to set up a defensive perimeter and eat for the night. We were outside the fence, sort of downwind of one of the corners of the camp. In the night some of our trucks came up with loads of K rations for the camp.

Then orders came down for us to assault toward Munich, to the south; we had another river crossing ahead of us. Lieutenant Fielding took prison camp photos on his 35-mm camera; I still have copies of some of those. We moved on, but we would never see another day like that day's history of horrors.

* * * *

Looking back, we were so hardened by death. We had seen so many dead bodies that it didn't impact us in the same way it does when I reflect back now. But through the years, I couldn't really talk about what I saw. There are no words; I can't explain it. The older I get, I am more aware of what really happened. Deprivation is too mild a word to describe how these prisoners were treated. They were given a can to use for their water, to eliminate in, and to eat out of, and were never able to clean their can. It was a horror, outright evil.

> LOOKING BACK, WE WERE SO HARDENED BY DEATH. WE HAD SEEN SO MANY DEAD BODIES THAT IT DIDN'T IMPACT US IN THE SAME WAY IT DOES WHEN I REFLECT BACK NOW. BUT THROUGH THE YEARS, I COULDN'T REALLY TALK ABOUT WHAT I SAW.

Most countries kill, but the Germans were beyond brutal. How any human can conceive this is unimaginable. Those poor people were beaten down in every way possible before they were killed.

After the war was over, Germans got mad if you brought

up the camps. They had to know. Even though they said they didn't, you couldn't get past the smell, the sound, the sights. I ran into a man some years later who had been in the Dachau camp and told him I was part of the relief. I was glad to know someone had survived.

At the time, I didn't think it affected me, but it did.

Outside the Utah Beach invasion museum
during my visit back in June 2014.

The B-26 "Marauder" Bomber in the Utah Beach museum. When the sun
shines through that roof, it hits the plane in an awe-inspiring way.

I'm at the museum, taking a break. Facing me is actor Ross McCall, who played Corporal Joseph Liebgott in the excellent TV movie Band of Brothers, which followed the path of the 101st Division, nicknamed "Easy Company." In the scene in which a concentration camp (not Dachau) is liberated, Liebgott/McCall is pulled from a patrol to help translate, in German, with the starving prisoners.

My friend and aide, Joe Machol, who runs WWII ETO tours, poses with actor Ross McCall, who played Cpl. Joseph Liebgott in Band of Brothers, in the Utah Beach museum.

*Joe Machol with actor James Madio, who played
Sgt. Frank Perconte in Band of Brothers.*

*The gate of the Dachau Concentration Camp, today a museum, which
we visited during my visit. The famous phrase, Arbeit Macht Frei, means
"Work shall make you free," and was posted at the gate of other German
concentration camps as well. It was, of course, a ruse, an outright lie, as
the Germans never intended to set these camp victims free.*

This plaque honors the 42nd "Rainbow" Division, which liberated Dachau. I'm visiting it in June 2014. It reads: "In honor of the 42nd Rainbow Division and other U.S. 7th Army Liberators of Dachau Concentration Camp April 29, 1945 and in everlasting memory of the victims of Nazi barbarism, this plaque is dedicated May 3, 1992."

Lt. Russell Fielding used his 35 mm camera to take these photos of the dead in railroad cars at Dachau. Horrifying images that never leave your mind if you were one who was there to see this.

Tyrol, Austria

Knee-deep into the war, I wasn't politically informed. I had no idea the fear and concern General Eisenhower, his staff, and the British had regarding the Nazis and the possibilities that they might set up a last-ditch stand in the mountains of Tyrol, Austria. So our high command moved the 7th Army, and we turned south to cover the threat of a new Nazi nation in those Alps, in Tyrol, Austria. We were in and around Salzburg on the Danube River at Linz. Up a long mountain road sat an abbey for the Benedictine monks. They were famous around the world for making Benedictine liquor. This cocktail was called B&B (Benedictine and bourbon) and was popular at the time. B&B would knock you on your ass after only three one-ounce drinks. Didn't matter whether you drank it in a glass straight or over ice; the stuff was just damn strong. Unfortunately, all the booze was gone when we arrived, and so were the monks. S.O.S as we would say: "same old shit."

The monastery was a round stone and brick building resembling a fort. It was as big as half the size of Yankee Stadium. A large parade ground was in the center with a big, single-gated entrance with a wooden door. The monks all had single rooms with a closet, a window, and a single light. A long hallway connected them together. We were to camp out here. At least we had electricity and some straw-covered mattresses, which beat the frozen ground or a wet foxhole. I opted to use my old blanket and the German flyer's jacket as a pillow.

I was awakened from a sound sleep by an attack of bugs. I turned on the light and saw an invasion of bed bugs running for cover. I threw that old straw mattress and bed out the window right then and there! After dusting my blankets off, I slept the rest of the night on the floor. The next morning the supply sergeant was handing out bags of DDT, a super new bug killer powder, yellow in color. The army used DDT on everybody, including in prisoners' hair and uniforms. Even though the windows didn't have screens, that was the end of the bugs. DDT did the trick.

Orders came down for a full combat patrol, requiring about forty men. We packed two-day rations, grenades, and extra bandoliers of 30-caliber. Up the mountains we climbed, then through a valley. We climbed for a day and a half on a forested slope. We were all in excellent condition, but this climb was a chore. Our lead scouts got in to a firefight with four German SS (SS was short for Schutzstaffel,

ORDERS CAME DOWN FOR A FULL COMBAT PATROL, REQUIRING ABOUT FORTY MEN. WE PACKED TWO-DAY RATIONS, GRENADES, AND EXTRA BANDOLIERS OF 30-CALIBER. UP THE MOUNTAINS WE CLIMBED, THEN THROUGH A VALLEY.

or "shield squadron"). We moved to envelop them and came out on a big, green high meadow. We killed three of the four Germans. I didn't even get a shot off. Three of us moved in on a nice log cabin. Breaking inside, we saw a man in German army pants and an undershirt sitting backwards on a wood-backed kitchen chair. He had cut his throat but had done a poor job of it, meaning he was slowly bleeding out, but not dead. One of our guys walked over to him and put a .45 in his mouth to help him out. *Bang.* It was over.

We kicked his wife out the door, where she lay sobbing. They had a good amount of food stored up, and we found sugar, flour, spices—and three boxes of one-pound Hershey bars, ten to a box. This wasn't an army item, so it must have come direct from the United States. We ate some before leaving, and carried some back.

LITTLE THINGS LIKE THIS MADE A HUGE DIFFERENCE. WE COULDN'T CONTROL MUCH, BUT WE COULD BE CREATIVE. NOW THAT I LOOK BACK, I SHOULD HAVE CHARGED THOSE GUYS A FEE FOR THE USE OF MY HORSE!

You can't imagine how high up that log cabin was in those Alps. We eventually took a road up to a valley that then led us out to a town about fifty miles from our camp. We had to climb back the way we came. This time, I decided to take a mid-sized horse with me. I got his bridle and took him along. He came in handy. Six of us hung our packs over that horse, giving us a lighter load. Little things like this made a huge difference. We couldn't control much, but we could be creative. Now that I look back, I should have charged those guys a fee for the use of my horse!

We continued walking and climbing for another whole day.

By nightfall, the tops of our toes and feet were worn and blistered. Talk about massive pain! Some of us had foot powder that helped a little. I used that old horse to lean on a lot, and he was a great aid to me. Going down, we stopped to eat and rest for the night. We were a mess for three or four days. After we arrived back, we never heard a peep about the shooting of that old guy. I will not go on the record, then, as being the one who told. Just suffice it to say that I wasn't the one shooting.

I never got to read the action report, and frankly, didn't have a right to do so. Most of all our fellows are dead now anyway. Or, as the 42nd Division says, "Over the rainbow." It only matters to those still alive now.

Postscript: The night after we got back from the patrol, I received a letter from my mom. She wrote that she was glad and relieved that I was safe now, that the war was over in Germany. Little did she know about things like this patrol. Nor would I tell her.

TRACK TEAM AND A WEEK'S PASS

And finally, the war was over. The Japs had surrendered; the troops were going home. The process took some time, however. Thousands of men from multiple divisions and all their equipment had to be shipped back to the United States. Thousands of American boys no longer had a mission to complete and suddenly found themselves rather bored. The transition didn't allow for much of a social life, and beer was in short supply.

So our group decided to host a track meet and call it an Instant Olympics. Each regiment put together a track team to compete, with a final race in September. The catch: events were done in GI boots! Those ankle-high, rough

EACH REGIMENT PUT TOGETHER A TRACK TEAM TO COMPETE, WITH A FINAL RACE IN SEPTEMBER. THE CATCH: EVENTS WERE DONE IN GI BOOTS!

leather, two-buckle boots weren't light. That meant conditioning, so a lot of guys started hopping around in their boots to get ready to race. Coaches were picked for our 222nd, and Colonel Luongo even got involved.

Events were the 100-yard dash, the 220, a half-mile relay, a one-mile relay, broad and high jumps, pole vault, shot put, and the javelin. Most every town had a ¼-mile track to use, giving us plenty of practice areas. I personally was not interested because my experience at school was in swimming and football; I had lettered in both. One day, I wondered over to the workout field, where this shirtless guy was practicing throwing the javelin. The javelin event takes a special skill of holding that spear, running with it, and throwing it. Javelins are a spear of wood with a steel front tip, usually well balanced, weighing about two to three pounds. The Roman army had large companies of spearmen, carrying and throwing javelins into the enemy at a very high arc so that they would come down *behind* the enemy shields. They would fly about 100 yards, or the length of a modern-day football field, which is a good distance!

I WATCHED THIS GUY FOR A WHILE, AND THEN THOUGHT I WOULD GIVE IT A TRY, AND ON MY FIRST ATTEMPT, I THREW IT FARTHER THAN HE DID IN ALL HIS PRACTICE THROWS! AS A RESULT, I ENDED UP ON THE TRACK TEAM BY DEFAULT.

The throwing technique was fairly easy, and I had done that in high school, but hadn't competed. The technique required you to hold the javelin in your throwing hand at the balance point while you ran about six or seven strides to the throwing line. You then would cast the spear forward, hopefully at the best-distance angle so it could sink into the earth downrange. I watched this guy for a while, and then thought I would give it a try, and on my first attempt, I threw it farther than he did in all his practice throws! As a result, I ended up on the track team by default.

Later on, they needed someone to run the 440 relay. I was a fast runner, so I got volunteered for that one, too. Over the course of several weeks, we worked out daily—in our combat boots. We ran in our OD undershirts and shorts with no jock straps. Everyone felt good and we rounded out our thirty-day conditioning system.

I placed second in the Division. Right before our final "Olympic meet," we were given real track shoes with front spikes. We even had light wool socks, white shorts, and shirts. They pinned numbers on our backs, and we felt like we were truly Olympians. It was quite a sight with all the different teams. I'm still not sure how the army pulled all that off. The spiked shoes took some getting used to. In fact, we kept tripping and falling until we became accustomed to them. We were just flying, emotionally, about all of this! I mean, the shoes were extremely light-weight, especially compared to our combat boots. They had four holes on each side and spikes about a half-inch long at the front, giving you a toe-up foot stance. The spikes sank into the soft sand of the track, providing a claw-like traction to start. Running in those shoes forces you to be on your toes, and it is actually tiring if you stand for too long. But our feet were about two pounds lighter, and that was amazing!

They trucked us into Salzburg, Austria along with half of our 222nd Regiment. We were confined by our platoons until the race. Our team did well, and we accumulated enough points to win the meet. Our 440-meter relay team took first. I ended up second in the javelin throw again! Our commanders were so pleased that they gave each member of the track outfit a week's pass to England in addition to the travel time needed to get there, which could take up to seven days.

We traveled by train from Tyrol through Paris to Calais, France, and then got on a ship to cross the English Channel. We didn't use tickets, but hitched a ride because the trains had avail-ability. Besides, we had buckets of invasion money (those French francs).

AUDREY . . . IN PARIS?

Getting from Innsbruck to Par-is took two full days on the Ger-man railroad. We carried our own food and slept in our seats. Some-times, fruit or bread was available for sale. We changed trains in Paris and decided to lay over, even if that meant staying up all night. We hopped on the underground rail, or metro as they called it, and found a world of wonder. Below Paris is a world of white tile, clean stations, and modern amenities. We headed for the red light district, which was by the Seine River. We drank plenty of wine, and ate wonderful goose liver paté with crackers and delicious French rolls. All types of lovely French women were around, and we talked with about all of them, asking what the going rate was.

I walked down the block to another tavern where, before my eyes, I was looking at my little girlfriend from St. Louis, Audrey Cushing, standing in a doorway! I couldn't believe it. Audrey was my steady girl of about a year back home. She and her fam-ily lived three blocks away from my parents' house. But back then, I never so much as felt her up; we were going slow. Kids

> I WALKED DOWN THE BLOCK TO ANOTHER TAVERN WHERE, BEFORE MY EYES, I WAS LOOKING AT MY LITTLE GIRLFRIEND FROM ST. LOUIS, AUDREY CUSHING, STANDING IN A DOORWAY! I COULDN'T BELIEVE IT.

were different back then. Couples didn't go around screwing each other or living together. Girls weren't getting knocked up like they do now. Back in my day, things were a little different. Our word was our bond, and we were held accountable by our parents. We didn't have all the drugs, or at least we didn't use them the way they are so rampant today. All that to say: Audrey and I took things very slow.

But now, in Paris, I just couldn't believe my eyes and what I was seeing. Was this the same girl from St. Louis in a Paris red light district doorway? She had the same build and tapered legs, which looked great in those high heels, with a stunning complexion and gorgeous brown eyes.

I walked over and called out her name: "Audrey?" She answered by telling me what she charged in francs. We settled for three American bucks.

So it wasn't Audrey, and I had to settle for imagining I was with my old girl as I made love to this stranger. When I returned home from the war, I learned that the real Audrey married a high school guy I knew. I never mentioned my Paris affair . . . ever.

Before leaving Paris, I went to a money exchange place to convert my invasion money from francs to English pounds. The pound was worth about $2.50 per dollar at the regular exchange rate, but on the black market it was at $3 to each of our dollars. Needless to say, we made out great. The pound notes were oversized bills. I had about two thousand dollars' worth, so it didn't fit in my pants pockets. We all had to stuff the money in our shirt pockets and in our jackets. Since we didn't have any travel or food expenses, we were sitting pretty.

A Wake-Up Call, and Some Golf, in England

I wanted to go to London and fool around, but Floyd knew

about a resort golf club outside of Bournemouth, just down the coast from our landing port, off South Hampton. We took a taxi over to the golf club, and they didn't want to let us stay. We were cleaned up and decent looking, I thought. We convinced them to let us stay a night, especially since our cab had already left.

The rooms included meals in their formal dining room, where the other guests got a good look at us. We behaved ourselves and met lots of British. They let us know that evening that because of a cancellation, we could stay. We each had our own room. They were all oak paneled and quite elegant. The only bad thing happened the next morning. Their customary wake-up was having the waiter key into your room to bring you hot milk and tea. He came in and shook us awake. Well, when he shook me that morning, he looked like a German in his waiter's uniform. I was on his ass in a flash. He was lying in the corner, milk and tea spilled everywhere. We explained what had happened to the management, and for the rest of the week, that waiter changed his wake-up routine with me. I got a simple knock on the door. That taught him to shake me!

> WELL, WHEN HE SHOOK ME THAT MORNING, HE LOOKED LIKE A GERMAN IN HIS WAITER'S UNIFORM. I WAS ON HIS ASS IN A FLASH. HE WAS LYING IN THE CORNER, MILK AND TEA SPILLED EVERYWHERE.

One day, we went down to the golf pro shop. We played eighteen holes on a course overlooking the English Channel. I played quite a bit of golf back home, and I enjoyed the relaxation and quiet at Bournemouth. The little old pro at the club helped with some instruction, and he sold me a set of clubs and canvas leather bag. They were a used set of clubs, but I was pleased with my four clubs—driver and three irons—and a putter.

I played with an American representative for Singer Sewing Machines. He had a good-looking blonde daughter who was married to a British solider who was still over on the European continent. One day, we played alone with her father. We came to a low place in the course, and she and I necked. She let me feel her up, but she was afraid of getting caught or knocked up. I'm not really sure which scared her more. Since she was in a completely different wing of the resort, she wouldn't come to my room. And that was the end of that.

The last night of our stay, I met with the chef and planned a party for the whole dining room, which was about fifty guests. We had beer, scotch, finger sandwiches, cheese, and more. I even had them make a cake. Sugar was difficult to come by in England still, but they pulled it off. The whole vacation stay and party cost me about $250. I was carrying thousands with me, so the cost was no big deal. You should have seen me back on the ship. Some of the guys were hooting at me coming down the gangplank with my golf bag and clubs.

THE WHOLE VACATION STAY AND PARTY COST ME ABOUT $250. I WAS CARRYING THOUSANDS WITH ME, SO THE COST WAS NO BIG DEAL.

It was back to the wreckage of war. Back to Paris and then on that German railroad to Salzburg.

This wasn't exactly like coming home, but it was good to get back to my outfit and pals. I think that was about the time we moved to Vienna for joint occupation with the English, French, and Russian allies.

VIENNA

From Innsbruck, Austria, we moved by truck to Vienna. This was a long trip in an open truck. Upon arrival in Vienna, we looked like dirt monkeys, covered with a coat of road dust. We got into a big block of nice apartment buildings, void of any furniture and rugs, so we just slept on the floor. It was a long way from, and infinitely better than, any foxholes, though. We were able to cook our own meal rations with our Coleman stoves. We shared occupation of Vienna with the British, French, and Russians. I still have my issued passbook.

We had little duty and sat on our apartment floor playing poker with captured German marks, of which we had thousands and thousands. In fact, we carried big bags full of loose bills. They were worthless to us. But our invasion money was another story. It was our wages and it served as black market currency. These 3-inch-by-3-inch stacks of bills (10s, 20s, 50s, and 100s) were money printed in the USA, I think. I know Roosevelt gave printing plates to the Russians, and they printed up a lot of invasion money. It was only worth 10 percent to them. In other words, our ten-dollar bill was only one dollar for the Russians. But we had a good time in a big park full of statues, where we found the black market for Austria. I retained some of the banknotes; they were in French francs.

Our primary duty in Vienna was simply this: standing at parade dress every once in a while. We cleaned up pretty good. One time, while we had duty guarding a coal yard, we did have an incident with a drunk Russian who fired his burp gun at us. As a result, I think he is still wearing that burp! That was the end of him. There was an officer inquiry, but we were found to have only done our duty. Two guys in our detail expended five 30-cal cartridges. I thought they wanted us to pay the army back out of our pockets with the way they were so mad about it back at regimental HQ. But the ironic thing was the Russians didn't care a bit; at least, that is what they ended up telling us.

ONE TIME, WHILE WE HAD DUTY GUARDING A COAL YARD, WE DID HAVE AN INCIDENT WITH A DRUNK RUSSIAN WHO FIRED HIS BURP GUN AT US. AS A RESULT, I THINK HE IS STILL WEARING THAT BURP! THAT WAS THE END OF HIM.

Not too far away from our apartments was the downtown ring and Karl's Platz; this is where the black market could be found. The Russians would buy anything: old boots, old raincoats, watches. We took plenty from the Germans prisoners, and the going rate of a watch was 100 bucks. Cigarettes cost us about 50 cents a carton, but we sold them to the Russians for a hundred dollars. We could then buy two or three cartons of cigarettes a week from the post exchange. I sent home about $2,500 in money orders. The army stopped allowing us to send our pay home, so we started storing up those small invasion bills. We had about seven to ten thousand in U.S. dollars per man.

Back home in St. Louis, you could buy a nice house for $7,000! Automobiles were about $1,000 to $1,500—if you could get one. We thought we were getting to be super-class citizens with plenty of means. It didn't turn out that way. I gave a postal clerk five thousand bucks to send home, and I even paid him money to do so. Well, I am still waiting for the money to arrive, some seventy years later! Apparently the clerk transferred out, and that was the last I saw of him. That was that.

I soon left Vienna with enough points to return home. I managed to keep $2,500 and had no trouble bringing home two pistols.

* * * *

People often ask about that point system. Here's how it worked in my case, as best I can recall it.

You received one point for each month of service in the U.S., so I had 30 points for my stateside time. You received two points for each month overseas: 28 more points, for my 14 months. You received five points for each decoration, or medal; thus, 20 more points. Now I'm up to 78. (Some of my decorations did come after my discharge.) And you received five points for each battle star; for me, another 15 points.

So that's how the math went, and you'd think the total was around 93 points. My recollection is that my point total somehow came to 87. But that was enough, and it called for my immediate return to the U.S. and separation from the Army.

Not long after, I went with the 45th Division on our long way home to the good, old USA. That concluded my second November and December in Europe.

RUSSIAN TROOPS

I remember when Russia was called The Union of Soviet Socialist Republics (USSR). But this came after the war. Political leaders at the end of World War II, including our President Roosevelt, Great Britain's Winston Churchill, France's Charles De Gaulle, and Russian's Joseph Stalin, agreed at the Potsdam Conference to occupy and divvy up Vienna like a slice of pie. A new map of the area was drawn. Our slice of the pie bordered on Russia's area. We had a good look at them as an army and as individuals. Coming into Vienna, we passed through their camps and army outfits.

We were camping outside one day when one of their divisions passed through our area. About 12,000 men; we were told it was a division from Russia, from Outer Mongolia. The individual soldiers looked like white Chinese. I know what Down's Syndrome looks like, and these Mongolians had the same flat face and altered head. Political correctness tells us that it's forbidden to say "Mongoloids" anymore, but they exist.

This Mongolian army wore flat, round helmets, pants, and quilted boots. Their outer cover was a long-sleeve smock. Their fronts were dirty with food and grease scraps. They each had a heavy belt around their smock at the waist, so all they had to do to take a dump was undo their belt and drop their drawers. Much easier than our setup.

They lived like dogs. In fact, they loved to *eat* dogs. After they passed through a town, no more pets were left, including cats. Just ask their victims, and they will tell you what I say is true. They raped every woman in their path. They carried submachine guns and old bolt-action rifles.

> THEY LIVED LIKE DOGS. IN FACT, THEY LOVED TO EAT DOGS. AFTER THEY PASSED THROUGH A TOWN, NO MORE PETS WERE LEFT, INCLUDING CATS. JUST ASK THEIR VICTIMS, AND THEY WILL TELL YOU WHAT I SAY IS TRUE.

Their transportation consisted of old-time farm wagons with wood wheels. They picked hay up along the way, moving at a snail's pace, less than two miles per day. Some were pulled by oxen, others by horses. The wagons were good for carrying loot and who knows what else. They reminded me of Attila's Horde. Passing them took our division days. They had first marched from Outer Mongolia, just above China, into Siberia. Some of the officers mingled with us, and we had been briefed on how to conduct ourselves by our company commander. We couldn't take any security risks, as we didn't know much about them.

We looked down on them, as they were pre-Civil War equipped. We didn't get too close to them, although we had a few conversations with them over tea in Vienna, where we sometimes gathered. They loved the black market and would often buy anything being sold. We heard the Russians were ready to buy Jeeps, guns, watches, and anything else they could get their hands on. Bob Swanson from the Second Platoon, who later became a professor at the University of Wisconsin, brought a picture of he and Boris Yeltsin, that was taken in Vienna, to a reunion. The Russians definitely had some handpicked persons to mingle with in those Vienna coffee houses.

I saw several Communist street parades where Soviet flags were flown, even though the war had just ended. With the dismantling of the Soviet Union, they dropped the socialist word. I warn you, though, they may call themselves socialists, but they are still Communists! Liberals don't like the word *socialist* because two and two still equals four.

Hitler was vaulted into complete power by the advent of the clever, exclusive use of radio. One radio in each home with one station was all it took. No one ever said Nazis weren't clever. So, whoever controls the media must be closely watched.

*This was my pass in Vienna. It's got my last name, and
it's in Russian, English, and French.*

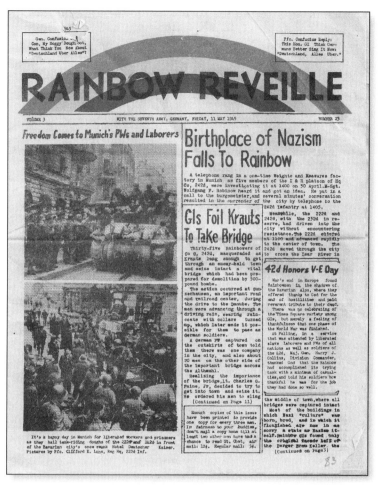

My copy of the Rainbow Reveille. It followed the Seventh Army, and is dated: Germany, Friday, 11 May 1945. Just imagine what had been accomplished. One year earlier, to the day, Germany controlled the continent, and the date was still about four weeks shy of the Allied invasion of France at Normandy. On the date of this publication, Germany was a conquered country.[4] Twelve days earlier, Hitler had committed suicide.

The photos at left of the cover page of the Reveille have this caption:

It's a happy day in Munich for liberated workers and prisoners as they hail tank-riding doughs of the 222nd and 242nd in front of the Bavarian City's once swank Hotel Deutscher Kaiser. Pictures by Pfc. Clifford E. Lohs, Reg HQ, 222nd Inf.[5]

And here's a read of one of the stories—reprinted exactly as written—on the front page of that Reveille:

GIs FOIL KRAUTS TO TAKE BRIDGE

Thirty-five Rainbowers of Co. G., 242nd, masqueraded as Krauts long enough to get through an enemy-held town and seize intact a vital bridge which had been prepared for demolition by 500-pound bombs.

The action occurred at Gunzenhausen, an important road and railroad center, during the drive to the Danube [River]. The men were advancing through a driving rain, wearing raincoats with collars turned up, which later made it possible for them to pass as German soldiers.

A German PW captured on the outskirts of town told them there was one company in the city, and also about 20 men on the other side of the important bridge across the Althmuhl.

Realizing the importance of the bridge, Lt. Charles G. Paine Jr. decided to try to get into town and seize it. He ordered his men to sling their arms, keep their heads down, not to talk, and to march into the city as if they were a group of Jerries heading for the bridge. . . .

. . . The ruse worked, the 242nd soldiers got in place, shot down several Germans who finally recognized who they were, and then positioned themselves near the bridge, quickly cutting the wires to the 500-pound bombs. The article ends this way:

. . . Back at the bridge, Krauts [still] tried to blow the structure, which would permit the Division to cross the river and push on to the Danube. One by one, six men attempted to reach the bridge and the bombs, which they apparently believed to be still wired, and each man was killed.

One other try at knocking out the bridge was made when a group of Jerries tried to push a cart loaded with dynamite onto it. They were stopped less than one block from the bridge. All members of the Jerry group were killed by a company which had been rushed to the aid of the patrol.[6]

The End of War

The trip back was long.

I know I will never get back home. Without question, this was how we felt through so many months of the war. But after the war ended in the spring of 1945, we started the mental process of regaining hope that we might actually get home. I can't tell you when it first started. All I know is we had trouble adjusting. During the war, we faced each day not knowing whether we would live or die. In retrospect, I guess we were all suffering from post-traumatic stress disorder (PTSD)—as it has now been called—but by varying degrees. We didn't have a label for it then; there was no diagnosis of such a thing.

We'd vacillate between sympathy for the dead to guilt for being alive. We'd act goofy or half mad—sometimes at the same time. The guilt for the deeds done weighed heavily upon us, but we are damn proud of having won the war, defeating pure evil.

All of this is turning around in our heads, and it can make one dizzy, to say the least. Our heads were not on straight when we returned home. No one's was; no way it could be. In fact, as I write this book, the images are vividly flashing before my eyes like it was only yesterday. I find myself reliving experiences and becoming upset, agitated.

I FIND MYSELF RELIVING EXPERIENCES AND BECOMING UPSET, AGITATED.

My points (see explanation in the Vienna chapter) got me home sooner than others in my outfit. We left Vienna by truck, then train. We got back to the "cigarette camps" by Reims in Northern France, a large city. (The Army called these transition camps cigarette camps, but there was no real reason for that name. Smokes really weren't any more or less prevalent in these camps than in other stops along the war. The camps just seemed to get that name; maybe it was because you could enjoy a smoke with far more leisure now that the war was over.)

At the camps, rows and rows of tents were put up, each holding about twenty men. The tents had canvas cots and a stove. November in Northern France is quite chilly at night. We were fed three meals a day and cold beer at night. We each had two blankets and wore our overcoats as well. One blanket went under our cot while the other covered us. Once the stove fire died out due to limited amounts of wood, the temps would get mighty cold—downright freezing! But still, these conditions were far better and more comfortable than being on the front line during battle. At least no one was trying to kill us!

Although the beer tasted great going down, it wasn't helpful in the middle of the night. All we wanted to do was stay warm, but we'd have to get up several times during the night to piss away those suds. We would postpone the call as long as possible because we would have to put on our pants, jackets, and boots to head outside to go. The latrine was a trench area three or four blocks away from the bunks. Armed guards were on duty 24/7 to ensure we didn't go near the tents. Can you imagine ten thousand guys pissing near your tent? The guards kept us honest . . . and clean.

Nonetheless, this did not deter us! We would stand in an endless line waiting for our cup of beer. We'd drink it down and go to the end of the line for another. The rules were one cup of beer per person at a time; no exceptions.

Newspapers were at a premium. We would place them under our blankets on the cot for insulation. They helped quite a bit. Nothing helped the thin army beer, though. It ran right through us! But hey, it was better than nothing. We certainly weren't complaining, and we appreciated the army's efforts. After all we'd been through, I know I appreciated it.

We were all being processed to be shipped home to the good old US of A. If you were sent to the Le Havre (France) port, you would be returned home via a five-day trip on the Queen Mary, crossing the Atlantic Ocean with speed and comfort. We were not that lucky, though. Instead, we were shipped south to Marseille, France, the same spot we had originally landed at and where the war began for us. We had a four- to six-week wait to get to one of those cigarette camps, with not much to do but wait. I helped out in the kitchen, as I knew my way around an army kitchen. I guess my multiple sentences via company punishment to KP (kitchen patrol) paid off. My buddy and I even carried potato peelers (the kind with the split blade and swivel handle) with us at all times. We could peel with the best of them, and we peeled a bushel of spuds like pros.

I didn't mind serving chow, as I would see someone I knew once in a while. I was always learning about food. Come to think of it, seems like I was always around food: getting it, cooking it, eating it, or serving it. People around me always ate better; we called it scrounging. We would get our hands on food one way or another.

One day while serving from the chow line, I saw a fellow I knew from high school. His name was Hank Banker, and he lived out on Halls Ferry Road, just a few miles from my home in North St. Louis. We had quite a time talking about our home, some 5,000 miles away.

Our trip by rail down to Marseille took about two days. We derailed and boarded an army troop ship called a victory ship. It wasn't too big and was modified to bunk and feed the troops. We boarded around noon on the key day with all of our worldly possessions in tow: guns, helmets, barrack bags, loot, and some memorabilia. We had pockets full of cash, and we each could bring back one pistol: a Luger, P38, or any foreign pistol not issued by the USA. We weren't searched or harassed one bit. They trusted that our company officers enforced the regulations, but those guys were too busy getting their own loot home to care about what we were taking with us.

> COME TO THINK OF IT, SEEMS LIKE I WAS ALWAYS AROUND FOOD: GETTING IT, COOKING IT, EATING IT, OR SERVING IT. PEOPLE AROUND ME ALWAYS ATE BETTER; WE CALLED IT SCROUNGING.

We got word that a big meal was being cooked for new passengers. The menu included fresh ham, mashed potatoes, and creamy gravy. It was all you could eat! Oh yes, I had seconds and thirds! It was the best meal we had eaten in more than a year! Everyone loaded up their plates as our ship departed and headed out into the Mediterranean Sea. The waves were fairly high, and the ship began to toss and roll. This was not a good combination! Everyone got seasick at once, and up came all those helpings of ham and mashed potatoes. I did not get sick, but most everyone was rushing to the fifty-four-gallon garbage cans. I saw one guy puke up his dinner and then get back in line to eat again!

For two days, that ham and mashed potatoes with creamy gravy sloshed around the decks. The ship's toilets were two inches deep in puke. Lord knows who ran that operation, but I felt for them. The next day, we passed through the Straits of Gibraltar and out into the Atlantic Ocean. The winter made for some stormy conditions, with waves crashing over the ship. We had to time our dash from one section to the other just right. We couldn't lie in our bunks, but we did get to watch some movies.

> AS I'VE SAID, I GOT SHOT THROUGH MY RIGHT HAND AND MY LEFT ARM, WHICH ARE STIFF TO THIS DAY. AMAZING WHAT A PIECE OF METAL FROM DECADES EARLIER CAN DO TO YOU.

We were aboard the ship between Christmas and New Year's Eve as we said good-bye to 1945 and welcomed in 1946. We landed at Newport News, Virginia, on January 2 and headed on over to Camp Gorden in Georgia, where we were officially discharged from the army. We were now among the world of civilians, a place where there was law and order. No more shooting artillery or setting off bombs. We could have hamburgers and chocolate milkshakes any time we wanted!

I called home and spoke with my mother on the phone. I noticed I could not hear very well, but didn't think much of it at the time. Years later, I realized that the war would leave me hard of hearing in my left ear. As I've said, I got shot through my right hand and my left arm, which are stiff to this day. Amazing what a piece of metal from decades earlier can do to you. I can't tell for sure, but I believe I have some splinters in my shoulder from my gunstock.

These are daily reminders that a soldier never truly leaves the battlefields.

After the War: Back Home in St. Louis

I'm often asked my feelings in regard to Post-Traumatic Stress Disorder (PTSD), which is talked about so much these days. I was diagnosed with PTSD in 1999, forty-plus years post-combat. It was a bit comical to me, and I am a bit cynical, to say the least.

I do not mean to sound jaded or insensitive, but what was the point of my diagnosis? I had lived with the flashbacks and reoccurring nightmares of my endeavors on an almost-daily—and nightly—basis. Sleeping with the lamp

> I DO NOT MEAN TO SOUND JADED OR INSENSITIVE, BUT WHAT WAS THE POINT OF MY DIAGNOSIS? I HAD LIVED WITH THE FLASHBACKS AND REOCCURRING NIGHTMARES OF MY ENDEAVORS ON AN ALMOST-DAILY—AND NIGHTLY—BASIS.

on in my bedroom when I could not sleep, or flinching when I would hear fireworks while sitting in my home, almost on a weekly basis (these occurred frequently from a local tourist attraction)—these things became my "new normal." What did the doctors think I had done all of these post-war years in order to be a contributing member of society?

Among the dwindling number of World War II veterans that still remain, I reside comfortably in my home in Seabrook, Texas, near Houston. I enjoy reading and watching the Military Channel in my spare time. On my encounters with various war/military articles that I come across, one struck me very personally recently. I read an article in the *Saturday Evening Post* magazine online, November 2014 edition. It summed up my feelings on not only what I had witnessed and endured, but also on how I dealt with my feelings on my return home to the states from Europe. The article, which I had only casually stumbled across, was titled: "On Films, the Comments of Kristin Tillotson." I didn't think twice about it after reading the headline, honestly, but what I read of the article? Afterward, it resonated to my core.

Tillotson is a film critic who typically writes for the *Minneapolis Star Tribune*. She wrote about the film Fury, directed by David Ayer and starring Brad Pitt, penning these words: "[*Fury*] is not just another World War II movie. It's perhaps less moving that *Saving Private Ryan*, but this bloody drama achieves something arguably more noble."7

These words had come alive on the page, and they kept playing in my head over and over, until I felt compelled to address exactly what and how I was feeling.

You see, I was very heavily judged when my beautiful and loving mother passed away in a warm and comfortable bed. I was completely devastated by her loss and just how much she meant to me. However, I did not feel capable of expressing any emotion at her passing, because it came in such a humane and dignified manner. After all, she had lived a very good and long life. Mama Havey passed at the ripe old age of ninety-eight. At that time, 1987, WWII veterans were not as sought after for their heroic story or as highly regarded as they are today, in my opinion. I had been called to duty to protect my country from horrific acts against humanity. I did not expect anything more from that than the freedom to live a normal life again upon my return.

I WAS COMPLETELY DEVASTATED BY HER LOSS AND JUST HOW MUCH SHE MEANT TO ME. HOWEVER, I DID NOT FEEL CAPABLE OF EXPRESSING ANY EMOTION AT HER PASSING, BECAUSE IT CAME IN SUCH A HUMANE AND DIGNIFIED MANNER.

Tillotson writes that steeping viewers in the brutal realities of combat and showing how war turned even some of the "greatest generation of heroes into numbed, conscience-free fighters," hardened the men charging into Germany, leading them to kill women and children, as nearly anyone was looked on as a combatant.8 All of this is very tough for a common person to comprehend. Being a part of the 42nd "Rainbow" Infantry Division, and a liberator of one of the most inhumane death camps imaginable, Dachau, it was and still is very difficult for me to accept—or to expect anyone else to remotely understand.

I continue to question the very existence of good in mankind after what I have witnessed. How could this happen? What is left for the "winner"? Is there a winner in this case, or is time the needed healer? Either way, I thank God that He is real despite all of this!

THE ST. LOUIS CARDINALS, DIZZY DEAN'S GOAT, AND A GOAT-NAPPING

Upon arrival back in St Louis after the war, it was hard to imagine, but life went on, it had to, and you had to find a way to fit in.

There was no such medical diagnosis in those days as Post-Traumatic Stress Disorder. But it was also just as hard to imagine the thousands of brave combat veterans thrust into civilian life after the horrors of long combat. (In my case, just twenty years ago as of this writing, the VA diagnosed me as a vet suffering from PTSD. "Stay within yourself," I believe, was the "answer" they gave us at that time to help us in dealing with our struggles decades after the war.)

Part of my course in retailing required clinical operations as sales personnel with the May Company, a famous bar in downtown St Louis. One of my classmates was Bill Saigh, a wonderful person who served in the Army, in Alaska. Bill's mother was from Lebanon and his father had passed away. Bill's brother, Fred, just happened to own the St Louis Cardinals professional baseball team. Fred Saigh was a wealthy, well-respected person about St Louis. Bill was the best man in my wedding to Shirley Eillerman, a Sigma Phi sorority queen of Washington University. Shirley was a real beautiful girl.

We always had box seats waiting at all the Cardinals' home games; Bill's job was head of concessions. Two teams played at Sportsman's Park, the St. Louis Cardinals of the National League and the St. Louis Browns of the American League. Each team's home games were scheduled while the other team was on the road. They traded off concession items by count when one team was on the road.

Dizzy Dean, a Hall of Fame pitcher for the Cardinals, by that time was retired and worked as the play-by-play radio announcer for the Browns. Dizzy was popular and loved by all the St. Louis fans; his Southern drawl and his stories about baseball tickled all of us as listeners in the Greater St. Louis area; there was not yet any TV in those days.

The St. Louis Browns baseball team, and Dizzy Dean fans, declared a special Dizzy Dean Day before a Browns home game at Sportsman's, which sat along Grand Avenue. This would have been about 1950. During the pre-game ceremony Dizzy received all kinds of gifts. Down on the field he stood: about six-feet-four, wearing his western hat, and waving with a big grin on his face. Among his Dean Day gifts was a goat: no kidding, a mid-sized white and brown Billy goat, given to him on a rope. The goat was good-natured and well behaved—but Dizzy had no place to feed the goat at his home.

Sportsman's Park was located midtown, northwest of downtown St. Louis. It was the only real ballpark in an old baseball town. As you walked up a zigzag rising passageway to the upper grandstands, each turn had a grassy area that was well-kept, providing real outdoor styling. And guess what? Well, this area is where Dizzy Dean kept, stabled, and fed his goat.

Bill Veeck had bought the Browns ball club, which was in the American League. Bill was the owner who had a midget bat in an actual Major League game. Fred Saigh, Cardinals owner, and Bill Veeck, in a word, did not see eye to eye, and this was on a number of matters.

Dizzy Dean's goat was taking all of this in—all while eating up all the lawn, bushes, and shrubs in his little area, and pooping all over to boot, causing an odor as Cardinals fans sought out their seats in the grandstands. Now, goat shit has a special odor, one that Fred Saigh didn't like. The goat in question would stand there looking up at the fans passing by, tethered to a twenty-foot rope that was badly twisted around. This went on for about three or four weeks.

It's my guess that Saigh and Veeck discussed Dizzy Dean's goat pasture more than a few times in these weeks, and how it was becoming a growing eyesore. Dean could not just toss the goat out because he had discussed and mentioned the blasted thing many times over his broadcasts, some of them national broadcasts, both in National and American League cities.

> BILL'S MESSAGE TO ME WAS SIMPLE: "BIRNEY, WE MUST GET RID OF THAT DAMMED GOAT."

Bill Saigh, my pal and the Cardinals' owner's brother, called me in for a very important meeting at the ballpark. Bill's message to me was simple: "Birney, we must get rid of that dammed goat."

So he and I started to plot. We laughed so hard we couldn't talk for a while. He had plans fairly well laid out since he was the last man to leave Sportsman's after all of the games.

Sportsman's was a large stadium, three tiers high and about

three city blocks long, and equally wide; it seated about forty thousand.

Under the outfield grandstands was a passageway where right field sat along Grand Avenue, a busy east-west street six lanes wide. There were storefronts facing Grand that housed various businesses and shops, with parking in front and a streetcar in the center of the road.

So the Bill Saigh and Birney Havey goat-napping plan went as follows: After a night game, Bill would lock down Sportsman's at about 1 in the morning. I was driving a new Kaiser automobile, a four-door black sedan. I removed the back seat so we could place the goat in it for a little ride. St. Louis in those days was a quiet city where we would leave our doors open and unlocked at night. At 1 in the morning there was little traffic, and this was especially the case on weeknights. Our goat-napping plan called for me to park on Grand Avenue, under right field, at the area where plenty of Stan Musial, Terry Moore, Pepper Martin, and Joe DiMaggio home runs sailed over. Bill was waiting for me with one of the storefronts open, a entrance leading under the grandstand passageway. We made our way under center field to left field to about the third base area, and then up the ramps to where the goat was tied up.

The kidnapped goat was glad to see us because I brought carrots.

We got the goat and his damned twenty-foot tangled rope, which was more of a problem than the animal, since it was all twisted up. Bill and I were laughing so hard we could barely walk back the way we came through the park. As we made our way back under the passageway under the stands and back to the storefront on Grand, we peeked out to see if the coast was clear. Wouldn't you know it, walking across the street was a women and kids about nine and ten years old. What they were doing walking along Grand Avenue at 2 in the morning I will never know. We waited till they passed and I opened the back door of my Kaiser sedan and Bill came out with the goat. The victim walked right out and got in the back seat, and I shut the door in a flash. That little boy, for some reason, looked back as we were loading the goat, and I heard him say, "Look mom, it's a goat." By the time the mom turned to look back, the goat was already in my sedan; all the mom saw was Bill and I standing next to my Kaiser. Once again, we nearly fell over laughing. From there, things went like a well-oiled military patrol. Except for that kid and the goat looking out the window of my car. One guy driving pulled up alongside at a stop sign and was staring. He stared and stared until we figured he and the goat were winking at one another.

We drove out to my house on Halls Ferry Road in the suburbs, an area that was somewhat secluded. I tied the goat to the fence by my wife's newly planted weeping willow tree, which was about five or six feet tall. Then I took Bill back to his car at the ballpark; the Browns were coming home to play the New York Yankees later that day.

DIZZY DEAN STARTED HIS BROADCAST THAT DAY ANNOUNCING TO THE ST. LOUIS AND NEW YORK FANS THAT "SOMEONE STOLE MY GOSH DARN GOAT."

Dizzy Dean started his broadcast that day announcing to the St. Louis and New York fans that "someone stole my gosh darn goat." He kept that up for three hours during the ballgame. So we really had to keep that goat under cover.

Well, my wife Shirley didn't get mad very often, but when she discovered the goat had just eaten her new weeping willow, she was really angry. I could not believe my eyes—the willow was almost gone. It was me or the goat—one or the other. Shirley was holding the hammer.

Dean was still yelling on the radio about his missing goat, so I used my military expertise to devise another plan to move the goat and save my marriage. Shirley had old maid aunts who owned about twenty-five acres bordering our house and property. They leased this farm to a nice little guy and his wife and kids. That family farmed it part-time and lived in the farmhouse. My plan was for this meek little farmer to take Dizzy Dean's famous goat and keep him on that farm; it's just that he didn't have a clue it was Dizzy Dean's goat or that a goat-napping had taken place. This little farmer did not have a radio, so he wouldn't have heard Dizzy complain and complain about the goat. Now with the Browns headed out of town and Dean heading out with them, and the Cardinals coming home and the goat gone, grass was once again growing and the goat shit was all cleaned up and Bill and I had pulled off a major crime!

Some thirty years later Bill Saigh, who had never got out of school, became the Dean of Men at the St. Louis University Business Department. He and I had some adventures in later years, but we had miles to go before then.

About three weeks after my meek farming friend got this goat, he came to me and said, "Mr. Havey, I can't keep this goat anymore." The goat was now on a new rope; he had chewed through the old tether, gotten out, and eaten the neighbors' lettuce patch and just about wrecked the guy's whole farm. His neighbor said he would shoot that goat if it got on his property again. The guy's name was Cooney Oxman, a truck farmer who sold his produce at the local market. My dad had told me about this guy when we would drive past the Oxman place in the 1930s.

I called Bill Saigh and we planned a trip about a hundred miles to the south, into the Ozarks hills down by the White River, to give the goat away to the first hillbilly farm that looked like it had a secure fence. We found it and we never heard about that goat again. Dizzy Dean finally shut up about his goat on those radio broadcasts.

And that ends the story of that gosh darned goat.

Bill and I also bought a little white pig and named it Shirley—but that is a whole other story for another time.

A Jewish Boy
Who Escaped
Hitler's Ovens

I wrote about our 42nd Rainbow Division capture and liberation of the Death Concentration Camp of Dachau. After we were in, many of the poor starving prisoners who could still walk raided and looted the German food camp storehouse. Hundreds of prisoners brought us large Number 10 cans of meat and potato hash to open for them. To get to the food, the prisoners were not allowed knives or any kind of tools to open the cans. So they brought them to their liberators to open for them. Using my jump knife that I carried on my ankle, I—and others—worked for hours opening cans. We did this in shifts because our hands became so sore. What memories . . . memories that will never leave me.

. . . Jump forward to 1984, back home 39 years after we liberated the Dachau Camp, and now 31 years ago as of this writing. As part of my restaurant equipment business, I had the opportunity to attend a baking school for a new production of breads and rolls; the plant was in New Jersey and called Adam O'Matic. It was founded by a man named Adam Boren.

The first day of school in the plant, along with about six other students, we were ushered into Adam's office, where he welcomed us. As he was speaking, I noticed a framed picture of a young boy, 12 to 14 years of age, wearing a striped prison suit with a matching round, striped hat. During a break I asked him in German, "Sie waren ein duetscher Gefangener?" or, "Were you a German prisoner?" Adam looked at me as if I may be a German guard, and he replied, "Ya." I asked him where he was a prisoner, and he answered: "Dachau." I could not believe my ears.

I told him my 42nd Rainbow Division had liberated Dachau and that I was there that very day. Adam remembered the opening of the cans of food that first day, the shooting, our tanks rolling into the camp, and all the excitement of being saved.

We talked for days. He cried when he told me the story of his dear mother and two brothers, who went to the ovens there at Dachau. He told me that one day they were just gone; his dad had been taken from their home in Berlin. The family was taken by boxcar train together to the Dachau Camp. Adam's trip to the oven was delayed because he worked in the guards' kitchen. The three days I was at his factory in New Jersey, Adam was never more than a few feet away from me; he followed me wherever I went.

After my group left the factory, Adam and I kept in touch through our respective restaurant equipment businesses. He and I were so busy, and half a country apart, that we lost track of each other. I am sorry I lost touch with Adam of Dachau.

Adam missed Hitler's ovens and went on to have a good life and most certainly contributed to the advancement of the instore baking industry.

I still have that very can-opening jump knife, in a glass case hanging on my wall with other WWII souvenirs, here at my home in Seabrook.

Oh, the things that knife saw in Dachau.

Air Show: Attending Wings Over Houston

Each year for the past six years I have been a guest hero in the Tent of Heroes at Ellington Air Force Base in Houston, Texas during the "Wings Over Houston" event. Officially, it's called the Legends and Heroes Autograph Tent, and we sign autographs for two days, with long lines of people; they have bought programs where our picture, and articles about us, appear.

The flyers, pilots, and men I appear with . . . it is overwhelming to me to think about their service and contributions to our country. It is almost beyond belief. Where did we get these men? Where do we get them from today? Men such as . . .

Bud Anderson, who flew a P51 Fighter in Europe. Bud shot down 17 German aircraft on two tours of combat flying. He named his P51 "The Old Crow." You can find Bud on documentary TV programs often. Bud is a true American hero, and there are very few like him.

Dick Cole, pilot of a B-25 Bomber. Dick was an unbelievable copilot to General Doolittle's raid on Tokyo. His was the first plane off the USS Hornet to bomb Tokyo in 1942. Dick's plane ran out of fuel over China, and he parachuted and landed in that country. He was taken by Chinese friendlies and returned to the U.S. Dick Cole is now 97 years old and stands up all day.

Joe Machol is my friend and an official in the Tent of Heroes at the air show. Joe is a member of the Texas National Guard. His father, **Lt. Col. Fred Machol**, now passed on, also appeared in the Tent of Heroes. Joe is an official in the National Football League and works games for the Houston Texans NFL team.

No one will be able to phantom, or even plumb the depths of danger or commitment, that men like this made for our country. They didn't serve in a single day of heroism, but served prolonged, day after day, week after week, month after month heroism for all of us.

The Air Show "Wings Over Houston" is a highly organized affair, and yet mostly run by volunteers and made possible by local sponsors. The Air Force displays all types of aircraft and flies some fantastic demonstrations, all of this done in view of very large and enthusiastic crowds.

The December 7th Pearl Harbor Air Raid event is exciting, with authentic Jap planes and bombs. The pilots fly in and out, re-enacting the infamous Pearl Harbor Raid.

At these events, we see some of the best pilots of the U.S. Air Force fly stunts of all types, and they fly the newest types of fighters and experimental aircraft. The whole thing is "heads up" for two entire days.

In Seabrook, where I live, we are not too far from Ellington Field; we often see and hear aircraft flying in during the week before the air show. Aircraft fly in from Scholes International Airport in Galveston, from a well-known museum in Galveston, and from other locations. What with the old WWII aircraft flying around, it makes for exciting times around my house.

And then comes the finest of our Navy, the Blue Angels. They fly the F-18 Boeings, painted that familiar dark blue with yellow striping. The Blue Angels were conceived as a recruiting tool, to enhance Navy and Marine Corps recruiting efforts, and to represent the U.S. Naval Service to the United Nations, its elected leadership, and foreign nations. These amazing representatives in the Blue Angels serve as positive role models and goodwill ambassadors.

You've never seen anything like the Blue Angels flying in a six-plane formation with wings, noses, and tails almost touching, roaring through the air at 500 mph with that white smoke trail surging behind. It's amazing to think that they're on the deck one minute and thousands of feet up the very next.

These pilots are highly trained and our best. When you see them in person on the ground, you're amazed at the skill and courage that come from these men. Each one flies with their lives in the hands of the others; no mistakes can happen—zero.

The show has really gained momentum over the years. It's quite a big thing around the Houston area, one of the best times of the year. The whole area is special when you consider the Johnson Space Center also is nearby. For myself and others, it begins with breakfast at the NASA Hilton before the air show begins not far away. We then have special parking and special golf carts to take us to our VIP spots in the Tent of Heroes. And again, each veteran has a table of his own for autographs and pictures.

It's an amazing time, and I am very honored to be a part of it year after year.

Returning to Wingen-sur-Moder: 69 Years Later

My killings of the Germans in that house on February 16, 1945 are forever etched in my brain. So when I saw a picture of a house in Wingen-sur-Moder, France, covered with snow, showing mortar bursts in the road, I recognized that structure immediately. The surroundings were more than familiar: this was the house where the shootings took place. We lost two good Americans, Crews and Barney, out of our company that day. Seven Germans lost their lives as well. Hell broke loose inside and out on that cold, bitter day.

My neighbor and friend, Joe Machol, here in Seabrook, Texas, is very active in Veterans Affairs. His dad was a colonel in the army, where he covered some of the same area where my 42nd Division fought. While alive, his dad was involved with vets and probably gave Joe the bug.

Joe is an outgoing person and involved in the Seabrook community. He serves as a timekeeper for the Houston Texans, our National Football League team. Joe is in his third year of forming a travel tour company, one that specializes in WWII tours to old battlefields and historical sites and cities, led by yours truly. Together, we have led two trips celebrating the D-Day invasion and have attended ceremonies overseas. The second one marked the 70th anniversary of D-Day, in June 2014. President Obama, along with the presidents of France, Belgium, and Luxembourg, attended, as did the Queen of England. Your humble author, Private First Class Havey, was escorted to the area in front of a crowd of thousands, and decorated.

* * * *

On my first trip back, in June 2013, we revisited some of the towns and cities where the 7th Army fought: Bastogne, Metz, Strasbourg, Wurtzburg, Schweinfurt, Worms, the Maginot Forts, Haguenau, and Soultz-sous-Foréts. We cut through the Vosges Mountains, which were now in full spring dress. Joe was driving a rented car for our long haul. Unfortunately, I had a cold and sore foot, making the trek even longer and more uncomfortable. Each small town we entered had one-lane streets where the locals, impatient behind us, wanted to get by. Joe would try to get out of the way, but then I couldn't see the signs, names, and numbers. This was the case as we approached the village of Wingen-sur-Moder. The town

WE STOPPED, AND I INQUIRED IF ANYONE KNEW THE LOCAL WAR HISTORY OF 1945. THEY KNEW OF MRS. LINDA BERGMANN, WHO OWNED A HOUSE AND SMALL MUSEUM IN THE TOWN, THEY SAID.

had changed . . . well, just a little bit, since the last time I saw it! It was modernized and more colorful. The pictures then and now are astounding.

On a Sunday during that trip as we passed through Wingen, I noticed some folks on the street by a floral shop. We stopped, and I inquired if anyone knew the local war history of 1945. They knew of Mrs. Linda Bergmann, who owned a house and small museum in the town, they said. She had history records. The kind folks at the floral shop called Mrs. Bergmann, and she immediately sent her husband over to get us. He took us to their home.

They were quite excited to talk to a war vet, but didn't yet know the connection of the 91-year-old man they were speaking with. They invited Joe and I to have Sunday dinner with their family. We thoroughly enjoyed them and their hospitality. After a nice meal, we were taken up into the hills, where some foxholes still remain, along with old German machine gun pits—pits about sixty-eight years old, as of that visit, still sunk in the earth. These particular German troops were from the Norway SS Division, said to be about 800 strong at that time in 1945. January 1945 marked the Germans' main assault in that area, called Operation Nordwind, where they overran the 79th U.S. Division. They captured and killed hundreds of good Americans. Nordwind marked the last major offensive of the Germans in the war.

> I REMEMBER THE DATES WELL BECAUSE CAPTAIN WATERS APPOINTED ME AS THE WITHDRAWAL GUIDE. I HAD TO LEAD MY COMPANY OUT DURING A WICKED BLIZZARD.

I checked the German machine guns' field of fire, and it was straight down Main Street. Mrs. Bergmann wasn't born before

BIRNEY T. "CHICK" HAVEY

WWII, but her museum had information about the battles around Wingen-sur-Moder. Our division arrived in the region on February 1, 1945, and stayed through February 16 to clean out the new group of German troops. I remember the dates well because Captain Waters appointed me as the withdrawal guide. I had to lead my company out during a wicked blizzard.

We marched through the night in snowy fields to towns that included Wingen-sur-Moder, where we were attacked on the morning of February 16, 1945. It was in Mrs. Bergmann's house that I killed three Germans and earned the Silver Star. How strange to find this exact house!

> IT WAS IN MRS. BERGMANN'S HOUSE THAT I KILLED THREE GERMANS AND EARNED THE SILVER STAR. HOW STRANGE TO FIND THIS EXACT HOUSE!

Anyway, after coming down from the hills behind the house to the backyard, we were taken into the house through the back door. It was then—looking around at the kitchen, the adjacent dining room, and the overall layout—that it hit me: this was the very house in which I fought and killed those Germans! The house where Crews and Barney died. All I could do was turn to Joe and say, "Uh oh." That's literally what I said: "Uh oh!" I was stunned by own revelation.

After regaining myself, I made all this clear with the Bergmanns. I pointed out to them where the dead Germans had fallen and froze stiff. I shared how we moved out the next day to advance our position. Mrs. Bergmann was amazed that I knew where each soldier had fallen, including our own. She recorded each spot on pictures taken back in 1945, in photos from before and after the battle.

* * * *

Joe and I left that Sunday evening; we were exhilarated. In all the small towns, winding roads, and insane traffic, we had found that *one house*, that death house, sixty-nine years later. As we drove, memories were fresh. . . .

. . . I recalled the identification process of our dead by the graves reservation officer (GRO). After a break in a battle, protocol—and just plain humanity—dictated that we identify a body if we could. Company officers and any survivors were to look at dog tags and faces in hopes of identifying the dead. Captain Waters and I each viewed our two dead, Crews and Barney. The bodies were stored in white mattress covers in a van, their boots sticking out. Once identified, we'd take their boots off and tie a tag to their toes. They were to be buried, temporarily at least, in the mattress covers, as we had no coffins on or near a battlefield . . .

. . . As we traveled that spring 2013 day, I drifted back to the present time and wondered, as I did many times, if those soldiers ever were reburied in proper coffins.

My cover image for this book shows the sheer volume of the fallen. General Patton lies in the graveyard depicted on the book cover. But one image I have never been able to get out of my mind is that of those bloody mattress covers.

After my amazing discovery, we left Wingen-sur-Moder. But it is as if part of me never left the battlefield.

THE USA VS. THE SAN ANTONIO GIRLS CHOIR

Seventy years after the Allied Invasion of Normandy, France, I was invited to the celebration by the governments of France, England, Belgium, and, personally, by the President of the United States of America, Barrack Obama, to the Normandy Anniversary commemoration. The celebration in 2014 was held at Colleville-sur-mere, Omaha Beach, American Cemetery. The crowds were enormous, and we were expected to be in our seats at 9:30 AM; the program would start at 10 AM. It took nearly two and a half hours to arrive because of the massive crowds.

All invited Veterans were greeted by an honor guard and required to sit in wheelchairs. About one hundred or so of us were seated on the main stage, where French President Francois Hollande and U.S. President Obama were to speak. Both presidents were about 45 minutes late, so U.S. Defense Secretary Chuck Hagel and U.S. Secretary of State John Kerry went through the group of Veterans, shaking their hands. After a long wait, the President's helicopter arrived about fifty yards from the main stage.

After much pomp and circumstance, French President Hollande spoke first. Most of the American Veterans did not understand French, but Hollande seemed sincere, so all went well with us. President Obama spoke about Korea, Vietnam, and his family's part in WWII. He then said it was about time that we all start forgiving the Germans; all of the Veterans groaned at that remark. Hitler was the main reason more than 55 million people were killed during WWII, and his forces had wounded many Veterans sitting right there on that stage. Some guy sitting behind me in his wheelchair yelled out "somebody get a rope!" I guess he didn't want to fall out of his wheelchair. I noticed he didn't have any legs.

Well, some of my Republican redneck buddies from around Paris, Texas did not want me shaking hands with a Democratic President on TV in France, but a chance at that occasion did not come up anyway. However, I was on French TV a lot. One vet jumped up and shook hands with President Obama, and when he came back to his seat, he said, "I just shook the President's hand." One wise guy in the back yelled, "Well, what are you going to do with that hand—wash it or lick it?" We all broke out laughing; that is a typical GI remark.

As I wore my Eisenhower jacket with all of my medals and decorations for this celebration, our honor guards wheeled us back from the historic ceremony, through the beautiful gardens and down the black pathways. We rounded a corner with an eight-foot-high hedge, and there was a beautiful group of children, 10 to 14 years of age, the girls with long red gowns and the boys in black tuxedos. This group stopped me and asked if they could sing for me. It was the San Antonio Children's Choir. A large crowd gathered around and the choir sang its full program just for me. I have never been so moved. I spoke with Doctor Thomas G. Hardaway II, director of the choir, and his wife, Dorene.

They told me of these children from San Antonio, and how they were asked by the U.S. and French governments to sing at the 70th anniversary of D-Day. They worked for two years washing cars, bagging groceries, and having bake sales to raise funds for the trip. They were 50 yards from the stage. However, sadly, their public appearance was canceled and their little hearts were broken, right then and there, five thousand miles away from their San Antonio homes. Why, they were right on the spot to go on stage, and they could have filled in the long wait time.

Why was their public performance canceled? While there may never be an official reason stated, it was whispered that the reason was because they were from Texas and not integrated enough.

Later, back home in Seabrook, Texas, I called Director Hardaway and spoke with the good doctor; essentially, he confirmed these reasons. Dr. Hardaway sent me a documentary of the choir's travels to Normandy, France, a video in which I appear a good deal, and it was indeed heartwarming. But that cancellation confounds me to this day.

EPILOGUE
MY OLD HELMET

I was recently called to be a guest speaker at the Emery Weiner Jewish High School here in Houston; it's located just off of Highway 610. The physical structure of the enclave was not only beautiful, but so were the people who filled the building. I was greeted with a hero's welcome, and this was my second appearance there.

For the first encounter at this school, I was asked to attend a memorial service for all those who suffered and died in the German death camps during World War II. I was beyond honored when I got to light a candle with a former inmate of the infamous death camp, Dachau, in Austria. This is the same camp that my 42nd Rainbow Infantry Division helped liberate at the end of World War II. Not only did this experience help me more greatly appreciate human life, it changed my life, as I knew it, far beyond any words I could convey.

The night before I was due to speak at Weiner for that second time, I contemplated what items or war paraphernalia I should bring to the event. I decided on my knife/bayonet for starters, as that is what I used to open countless cans of German army food taken by the starving death camp inmates. They acquired the canned food during the liberation by raiding their capturers' rations stockpile. Not only was the sight of starving and dying people profound for a young man, I was taken back by the fact that these people had no means of opening their Heaven-sent windfall of food. Food . . . something they had been praying for, and something that we do not always think about not being able to acquire.

The second item that I decided to bring was my original

World War II helmet. If only this helmet of mine could talk, the stories it could tell. That old covering was with me through every single battle, including The Battle of the Bulge, the Battle of Northern France, and the invasion of Germany. This helmet was with me and I relied on it for more than six months of constant combat. However, even with all of that, the most profound experience that old helmet encountered was the capture and liberation of Dachau.

The smoke, dust, and stench of burnt human flesh and hair, and the sheer corruption, was like a cloud upon entering that camp. I remained at the camp for the better part of one and a half days. Now, as I looked at my helmet hanging on the wall of my comfortable home, seventy years later, I realized that there had to be some residuals from Dachau. You see, my helmet was never officially cleaned or washed in any way. It was at that moment that I realized my helmet must have been—and continues to be—a direct conveyor from my time at Dachau, even if just in the DNA it carries. It was the conveyor of evil and death and witness to all that I had experienced. Again, if it could only talk . . .

> THIS HELMET WAS WITH ME AND I RELIED ON IT FOR MORE THAN SIX MONTHS OF CONSTANT COMBAT. HOWEVER, EVEN WITH ALL OF THAT, THE MOST PROFOUND EXPERIENCE THAT OLD HELMET ENCOUNTERED WAS THE CAPTURE AND LIBERATION OF DACHAU.

As I continued to prepare for my second guest speaker appearance at this school, I decided that my French knife, bayonet, my helmet, and a handful of original photos from Dachau, 1945, were all I needed to bring for display and points of observation. At the conclusion of my interview, I asked the audience if they would like to touch my helmet—not a single one of them would. Was it the fact that their ancestors' ashes may, quite possibly, remain on it, or was it the single fact that it was witness to so much hate? I'm not sure I'll ever know why they all declined.

Later, following the talk, as I hung my helmet back in its place on the wall, I could not help but pause and think of its content, the impact of its being, and

AT THE CONCLUSION OF MY INTERVIEW, I ASKED THE AUDIENCE IF THEY WOULD LIKE TO TOUCH MY HELMET—NOT A SINGLE ONE OF THEM WOULD. WAS IT THE FACT THAT THEIR ANCESTORS' ASHES MAY, QUITE POSSIBLY, REMAIN ON IT, OR WAS IT THE SINGLE FACT THAT IT WAS WITNESS TO SO MUCH HATE?

then all of those experiences of my short time in Dachau came flooding back to me in an instant, all through that helmet. The remaining dust and ash on the piece of my uniform that protected my head . . . no matter how minuscule, those things still remain, right there on my helmet, now hanging on my wall.

The house and street in Wingen-sur-Moder, France, where we fought those Germans, and I killed three—1945 on a snowy day (top), and now. I was awarded the Silver Star for that battle, February 16, 1945. If you look closely at the top photo, you can see some circled numbers. These are where Mrs. Linda Bergmann, owner of the house today, marked where dead soldiers were found following the 1945 battle.

I'm looking at photos Linda Bergmann has on her wall, from the battle and war, during my 2013 visit back. Mrs. Bergmann is in the middle; that is her son on the left.

Getting ready to go up in a light aircraft, in France, June 2013, to review the area of some of our battlefields.

*I'm at Lt. Gov. David Dewhurst's house for a reception and din-
ner, in 2013. I'm at right, David at left. David's dad flew a B-26
Bomber in World War II, and the Dewhurst family helped with
some of the funding of the Utah Beach Museum, including a B-26
Bomber housed in the French musee.*

*Souvenirs taken from Germany at the end of World War II now hang
on the walls of my home in Seabrook, Texas. Each item tells a story.
Included are my helmet and M-1 rifle, along with my jump knife, other
knives, and much more. The money in the lower center frame is from
various countries we were in. We had a lot of marks from Germany.*

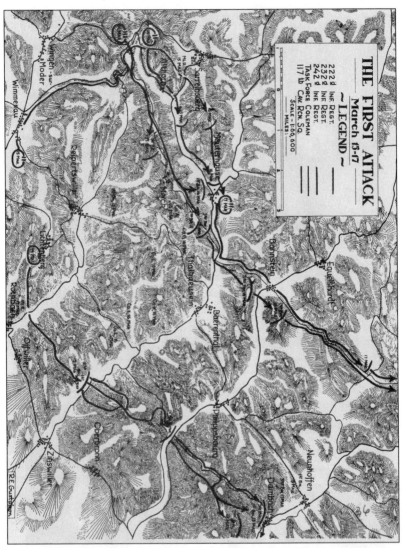

*A map of "Task Force Linden," which was commanded by Brigadier
General Henning Linden, an assistant division commander of the 42nd.
Task Force Linden was comprised of three infantry regiments in the
Marseilles, France region that successfully defended the area and kept the
Germans from breaking out of the Alsace. It defended a 30 mile-long front.*

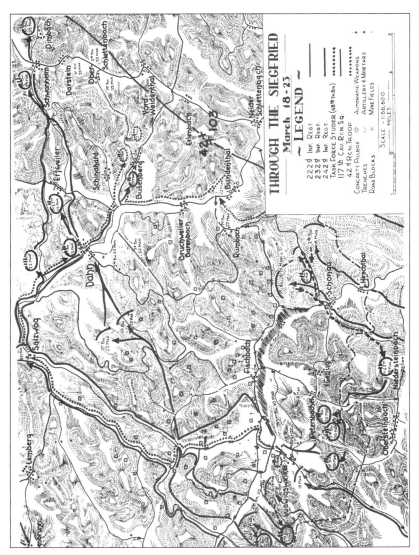

Through the Siegfried: the 42nd broke through the vaunted Siegfried Line and on into Belgium and Luxembourg. The actions took place from March 18-23, following the first map, above. Battle maps were drawn up just like this. The route of our 222nd Infantry is on this map. The map is scaled to cover about 15 miles from west to east.

A San Antonio children's choir serenaded us as part of the 70th anniversary ceremonies of D-Day, June 6, 2014. I got to listen to them up close, and pose with them. These ceremonies were held at Omaha Beach.

On the occasion of the 70th anniversary of the landing in Normandy

The Honorable Barack Obama
President of the
United States of America

His Excellency François Hollande
President of the
French Republic

request your presence at the commemoration ceremony

which will take place at the Normandy American Cemetery and Memorial

in Colleville-sur-Mer the morning of Friday, June 6, 2014

Guests are requested to be in their seats no later than 9:30 a.m.

Veteran

The copy of my invitation to the 70th anniversary event at Normandy, June 6, 2014. The invitation is from U.S. President Barack Obama and French President François Hollande. The event was held at the Normandy American Cemetery in Colleville-sur-Mer.

To Mr. Birney T. Havey
With best wishes,

*Photo from President George W. Bush (43rd President)
and wife Laura, thanking me for my service.*

September 3, 2009

Mr. Bernie Havey
2201 Nassau Road
Seabrook, TX 77586

Dear Mr. Havey,

Thank you very much for agreeing to participate in the *Testimonies from the Holocaust* oral history project with Holocaust Museum Houston.

Your oral history is an invaluable resource for future generations to have access to history, as well as a safeguard against revisionism. Through this project, your experiences will be committed to permanent memory and accurately preserved on video.

Your interview will take place at the Rice University Media Center in Houston, which is located on University Blvd., Rice University Entrance #8. Please plan to arrive 30 minutes prior to the recording.

The interview will last between one and three hours. It will focus on your experiences during the Holocaust. If you have any pictures, documents or other memorabilia from that period, please bring them along.

Due to several oral histories being conducted in September, I hope to schedule your interview in October or November. I will contact you to discuss scheduling the interview on a day that is convenient for you.

Please call me if you have any questions at 713-942-8000 ext. 110.

Sincerely,

Monica Rose
Director of Library and Archives
713-942-8000 ext. 110
mrose@hmh.org

In 2009, the Holocaust Museum of Houston sent me a thank you note for my contributions to their work. I took part in the Testimonies from the Holocaust oral history project. My interview with project historians took place at Rice University.

September 28, 2012

Birney T. Havey
2201 Nassau Drive
Seabrook, TX 77586

Dear Mr. Havey,

Enclosed please find the photographs you sent to the Institute for Oral History. I want to extend my sincerest thanks to you for taking the time to find and mail these images for use in the project. These photographs assist in allowing us to offer a complete record of your experiences during the World War II for posterity.

Those of us at the Baylor Institute for Oral History and the Texas Holocaust and Genocide Commission would like to offer our sincerest thanks for your continued participation in the Texas Liberators Project and we are happy that we are able to preserve your story for future generations.

Sincerely,

Stephen Sloan, PhD
Director, Institute for Oral History
Baylor University

Enclosed: Photograph

INSTITUTE FOR ORAL HISTORY
One Bear Place #97271 • Waco, Texas 76798-7271 • phone: (254) 710-3437 • fax: (254) 710-4659 • website: https://www.baylor.edu/oralhistory

103

Just three years ago, Baylor University, via Stephen Sloan, director of the Institute for Oral History at the university, sent me a thank you letter for photographs I sent that help preserve the awful history of the Holocaust. The photos aid the work of the Texas Holocaust and Genocide Commission. My unit helped liberate Dachau camp in late April 1945.

All of this war memorabilia hangs on the walls in my
home in Seabrook, Texas. Every item tells a story.

Army Paratrooper Jump Wings

Combat Infantry Badge

| *Silver Star* | *3 Bronze Stars with "V" Devise* | *The Purple Heart* | *The Army Good Conduct* |

| *American Campaign Medal* | *European African Middle Eastern Campaign Medal with 3 Battle Stars* | *Victory Europe Medal* | *Occupation Germany Medal with Germany Clasp* |

42nd Rainbow Division Patch   *Third Army Patch*

Expert Badges Chick earned

Presidential Unit Citation

U.S. Army Symbols and Abbreviations: 1944-1945

A few of these are as best I can recall them! — B.T.H.

KP — Kitchen police
CP — Command post
HQ — Headquarters
OD — Olive drab (color of uniform)
MLR — Main line of resistance
OP — Outpost
LP — Listening post (usually with field phones)
CO — Commanding officer
DL — Demarcation line
Capt. — Captain (an officer)
Lt. — Lieutenant (an officer)
Corp. — Corporal
G — Guide
Gen. — General (an officer)
Sgt. — Sergeant
Mi. — Mile
Mil — Military
LZ — Landing zone
LD — Line of departure
WP — White phosphorous (grenades)
HE — High explosive
AT — Anti-tank
Co. — Company (or, C.)
A. Co. — Alpha Company
B. Co. — Bravo Company
C. Co. — Charlie Company

D. Co. — Dog Company
E. Co. — Easy Company
BN — Battalion
Div. — Division
Regt. — Regiment
Corp. — Core
Gen. HQ — General headquarters
Mm — Millimeter
Cal. — Caliber
PX — Retail store or post (short for Post Exchange)
WIA — Wounded in Action
KIA — Killed in Action

NOTES

1. From "The Story of the Rainbow," *42nd Rainbow Infantry Division: World War II History*, Army and Navy Publishing Company (Kirkwood, Missouri: Messenger Printing Company, 1946; reprinted June 1979, July 1997, July 2004).

2. Ibid, p. 26.

3. Ibid.

4. Cover image, caption, and article are from *Rainbow Reveille*, Volume 3, Number 23, printed in Europe, May 11, 1945.

5. Ibid.

6. Ibid.

7. *Minneapolis Star Tribune* movie review. Read Ms. Tillotson's review at: http://www.startribune.com/entertainment/movies/279461392.html (latest update posted October 17, 2014; accessed December 23, 2014).

8. Ibid.